Henry Haversham Godwin-Austen

Land and Freshwater Mollusca of India

Including South Arabia, Baluchistan, Afghanistan, Kashmir

Henry Haversham Godwin-Austen

Land and Freshwater Mollusca of India
Including South Arabia, Baluchistan, Afghanistan, Kashmir

ISBN/EAN: 9783744761574

Printed in Europe, USA, Canada, Australia, Japan

Cover: Foto ©Andreas Hilbeck / pixelio.de

More available books at **www.hansebooks.com**

LAND AND FRESHWATER MOLLUSCA

OF

I N D I A,

INCLUDING

SOUTH ARABIA, BALUCHISTAN, AFGHANISTAN,
KASHMIR, NEPAL, BURMAH, PEGU, TENASSERIM,
MALAY PENINSULA, CEYLON, AND OTHER
ISLANDS OF THE INDIAN OCEAN.

SUPPLEMENTARY TO MESSRS. THEOBALD AND HANLEY'S

CONCHOLOGIA INDICA.

BY

Lieut.-Colonel H. H. GODWIN-AUSTEN,
F.R.S., F.R.G.S., F.Z.S., &c.,

LATE DEPUTY SUPERINTENDENT TOPOGRAPHICAL SURVEY OF INDIA, IN CHARGE OF
THE KHASI, GARO, AND NAGA-HILLS SURVEY PARTY.

VOL. III.

Part I.—NOVEMBER 1920.

LONDON:
TAYLOR AND FRANCIS, RED LION COURT, FLEET STREET.

1920.

ALERE FLAMMAM.

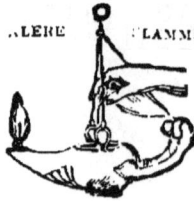

PRINTED BY TAYLOR AND FRANCIS,
RED LION COURT, FLEET STREET.

LAND AND FRESHWATER MOLLUSCA

OF

INDIA.

VOL. III.

Part I.—NOVEMBER 1920.

(Plates CLIX.-CLXV.)

INTRODUCTION.

In spite of the very limited interest which is taken in the animals of the land mollusca, I am induced to commence Volume III. of this work; for until the species in the many Oriental genera are collected, their anatomy made known, and their true habitat recorded, any attempt to use them for classification or any deeper research is not possible. The work of the Conchologist is simply useless unless this is done and the physical features of India are taken into account. During the war I have not been able to carry on this publication, begun 37 years ago and ended in two volumes in 1914. On the other hand, I have had leisure to do much with the material in my hands, and to add to it, especially specimens preserved in spirit, and have described the animals of many Indian Genera previously unknown. I have had much support—more than I had hoped to receive—and from many quarters : for this I cannot express my thanks too strongly. I must especially notice Dr. N. Annandale, with Messrs. S. W. Kemp and F. H. Graveley of the Indian Museum. I feel it a duty to those who have supplied material, to put what I have brought to light on record, as a starting-point for those who will follow me in this wide and difficult field of research, so full of deep interest to anyone who enters it.

I am most fortunate in having as a neighbour Mr. J. S. Gladstone, an excellent and skilful photographer. Without his valued aid I could not give the figures of types and shells from typical localities, which show far better than any description the direction their subtle differences take. For instance, how distinctly photography shows the difference between *G. tenuispira* of Teria Ghat (Plate CLIX. fig. 3) and the species for long regarded as the same from Sikhim (Plate CLIX. figs. 1 & 2). Mr. Gladstone made photographs of 60 shells, which fill three Plates. I may say here, but for this generous assistance, the publication of this Monograph would not have been possible. As an example of Zoological Research it has been met, and by private means alone.

Genus GLESSULA.

WHILE I have been studying this genus, particularly the animal, as specimens were slowly obtained in spirit, knowledge of its taxonomy has increased. This has led me to look at many species very closely, for much had been left incomplete by Colonel Beddome, particularly the species from the North-East Frontier of India, of which I possessed a very fine series.

Some of this work on the genus *Glessula* might have been published long ago in the second volume of the 'Fauna of British India'—some of it, anatomical, had been done ready for it; but I found I could not, under the conditions in which I was expected to work, complete it in time. I had reached an age when extra correspondence was to be avoided, when independent conchological work was pleasanter to do. It was not to be expected I could place my collection at the service of others, neither could I hand over original work on the animals of the genus on which I had spent so much time and expense during many years. I could not give the public the run of collections I had deposited in the Natural History Museum under certain well-defined and very reasonable conditions, reserving to myself the right to work on them during my lifetime.

At the end of Vol. II. (p. 435) I mentioned the genera I was engaged upon and trusted to deal with. Of these *Glessula* has been completed and is now presented in Part I. of this new volume. The anatomy of several species has been made known, and, when working out the collections made when the punitive expedition entered the Abor country and the Tsanspu Valley (1911-12), I took the opportunity of publishing the anatomy of a new species from Sikhim to elucidate that of the genus, as I did not see at the time, with the war going on, any chance of publishing it at all. The animals of other genera have come to hand and have been described and figured in the following order : *Anadenas* and *Opeas* (both very well represented in my collection), *Sivella*, *Harpalus*, *Planispira*, and *Plectotropis* (many species have been worked out in these four genera).

Among the earlier writers on *Glessula*—Pfeiffer, Benson, and both Henry and William Blanford—Geoffrey Nevill undoubtedly has the highest claim to notice ; he had made a special study of the genus, and knew it better than anyone I have come in contact with. Much of Beddome's knowledge was obtained from him in correspondence and exchange of specimens from Southern India. This is well shown in his copy of the ' Hand-List,' being a catalogue of all the Gasteropoda in the Indian Museum when his health compelled him to retire. This is not a mere reprint of the first original edition of 1878 containing 338 pages, but there is added to every species the work in which it was originally published ; all additional species (in this genus 28) are given with descriptions of those Nevill considered new, while in hundreds of cases throughout the book the dimensions of type shells are given. One point which must not be forgotten is Nevill's great accuracy in the records of habitat and the collectors through whom the species were obtained. The title-page is headed " Proof for new Edition," " For the Trustees Indian Museum—G. Nevill, 1-11-81." On another page, " To be offered to Trustees Indian Museum if they consider it may be of any practical value to them : if not, to be given to Col. Godwin-Austen.—Signed, G. Nevill, London, July 5th, 1879." Shortly after Nevill's death at Davos in Switzerland, I received the copy with other books and valuable notes, and did all I could to get it published.

On 23rd December, 1885, I first approached the Trustees of the Indian Museum, strongly advising the publication of a Second Edition ; in February 1886 I received a reply from the Honorary Secretary, Mr. H. B. Medlicott, of which this is the concluding paragraph : " The Trustees consent to your keeping present custody of and using the valuable copy of the Hand-list of Mollusca containing Mr. Nevill's notes and additions. There is no immediate prospect of special work in that branch of the collections." In fact, the post which Nevill held has never been filled up to this day : for 40 years the collections of Mollusca have been in many hands, and in the course of many moves some species catalogued by Nevill could not be found when I have applied for them. It says much for those who have had charge that the collection is not in a worse state.

I next took the book to Dr. John Anderson, the retired Superintendent of the India Museum, under whom Nevill had served. He could effect nothing, although, if I remember right, he went to the India Office : it was the old story—no funds !

In 1885, in a final attempt to see it through the press myself, I obtained from Messrs. Taylor & Francis an estimate for 672 pages, 500 copies unbound, £221 10s. 6d. This sum was not to be got—I had it not to give, but would have given what knowledge I had towards publication.

Much has lately appeared in the public press on "Research."
It is of interest to put a case like this on record (if only to show how
valuable scientific work and knowledge is lost for ever for want of
Government support.)　To show how research is valued and
rewarded, Museums are built at an enormous known cost and filled
with specimens at an enormous unknown cost; then a proper
scientific Staff to deal with them is grudged, expenses are cut down,
and the record is never utilized.　In this instance Nevill lost the
credit which many years of close study should have brought him—
not among those he had worked with, but among the general public.
I am glad I have the opportunity of bringing his labours to notice.

The best account of the genus is to be found in the 'Manual of
Conchology,' ser. 2, xx. 1908, commencing p. 50—the excellent
work of Dr. Henry A. Pilsbry, with copious good illustrations, not
only of the shells, but of the sculpture and of the embryonic apex.
He says (p. 52):—" From the purely conchological standpoint we
may be said to have an extensive knowledge of *Glessula*, yet various
characters of the first importance have been neglected.　*The
embryonic whorls of the types must be all re-examined, and their
sculpture described.*　Our ignorance of the embryonic sculpture of
many forms prevents any natural classification of the species.
The surface of the later whorls in all the species should be
examined under high power, since some species have a minute
sculpture not visible with an ordinary lens."　Further on, he
adds : " No natural classification of the species of *Glessula* can be
attempted until the sculpture of the apices of the shells and
the anatomy of a number of representative species are studied."
Bearing this truly excellent advice in mind, I have endeavoured to
follow it when describing the many species of the genus now known
from the Eastern Frontier of India and Burma.

Pilsbry * has given a good *résumé* of what has been done in this
genus and all that was known of the anatomy at that time.　For
this last we are indebted to the research of Professor C. Semper,
who published, in his ' Reisen im Archipel der Philippinen,' 1873,
p. 133, pl. xii. figs. 14–16 to pl. xvi. fig. 19, an anatomical description
of *Glessula orophila*, Benson, said to have come from Madras,
but it might have been collected in any part of Peninsular India.

It is unfortunate Semper's determination is open to doubt : we
shall never know whether the shell of the animal he dissected was
compared with the type of Benson's *orophila*, or what has become
of that type described by Reeve.　The species is not recorded in the
' Conchologia Indica,' so Hanley never could have seen it.　There
are no specimens assigned to *G. orophila* in either the William or
Henry Blanford collections.　Beddome records the species from the
Anamullay Hills; South Canara; Golconda Hills, east side of
the Madras Presidency, and says, " My Golconda specimens were
labelled by H. Nevill *G. subbrevis*, but I cannot see how they

* Man. Conch. ser. 2, xx. 1908, pl. xviii.

differ." Nevill, I think, only saw young examples ; Reeve's figure copied by Nevill (*i. e.* G. Nevill), is good.

Geoffrey Nevill, in a paper on new or little-known Mollusca of the Indo-Malayan Fauna *, gives a description of the shell. He writes, under *Stenogyra* (*Glessula*) *orophila*, Benson MS.:— " Reeve, Conch. Icon. 1850, fig. 105, anfr. 7, long. 14 mill., as *Achatina orophila*, Nilgiris and Colombo ; *fide* Pfr., = his *A. ceylanica*. I give a copy of Reeve's original magnified figure of his *A. orophila*, as I am by no means convinced Dr. Pfeiffer is right in uniting it to his *A. ceylanica* ; to judge from the figures, I should say they were quite distinct species. It may be that Reeve confused two distinct forms—the one figured (probably from the Nilgiris) a good and distinct species, the other from Ceylon a mere variety of *St. ceylanica* which may have been sent or shown to Dr. Pfeiffer as *A. orophila* and caused him to unite the two species. I have not myself seen any species of the group, *St. nitens, ceylanica, punctogallana*, etc., from Continental India."

Semper shows all the interesting details of the genitalia of his *G. orophila*, especially what he terms the flagellum, which is of very peculiar form, elongate and comb-like, a character thus typical of the genus. It is, I consider, the sac in which the spermatophore is developed. In the teeth of the radula the shape of the marginals is not given.

The genus, as recently as 1914, has been treated by Mr. G. K. Gude in the ' Fauna of British India.' He approached it with a great knowledge of conchology, bibliography, and especially synonymy—the last most useful to workers, but unattractive. They have to thank Mr. Gude for undertaking such labour. It shows, like so much work of its kind and of the series to which it belongs, that he had never been a collector in India and knew little of its physical features and all that that comprises. There is an absence of original matter, such as Dr. Jerdon, the Blanfords, Lydekker, Oates, Day, and others brought to bear on and embellished the history of the Mammals, Birds, and Fishes of India which they had collected and which had passed through their hands.

It is easy to find fault, and it may appear I do so with Gude's work. I am only animated by the desire and striving to make the record of Geographical Distribution as correct as possible ; thus under *G. tenuispira*, p. 379, I notice all the errors of determination which Blanford, Theobald, Nevill, Beddome, and myself have perpetuated. I have to point out that these determinations were made 40 to 60 years ago, much too long ago for such data to be reliable. I am able to say they were often made without sufficient material at hand, or on shells erroneously named in the first instance. I take, for example, *G. baculina*, p. 379, Khasi Hills (*Godwin-Austen*), evidently on the authority of Nevill in the ' Hand-list,' p. 170. It is a distinct species, which he did not notice ; I have named

* J. A. S. B. pt. i, 1881. p. 137, pl. v. fig. 10.

it *subbaculina*, for I cannot find in my collection from the Khasi Hills any *Glessula* that matches the type in the Henry Blanford collection.

Classification and Distribution.

Mr. G. K. Gude, in the 'Fauna of British India,' puts *Glessula* into the family Ferussacidae (p. 373), immediately following the genera *Cœcilioides*, type *acicula*, Müll., *Geostilbia*, type *caledonica*, Crosse, and *balanus*, Reeve, together with a new species, *G. bensoni* (p. 375).

With these genera I cannot agree that *Glessula* has affinity; the animals are unknown, the shells very different, the conditions of life and extent of range very distinct. Range is an important factor in questions of this kind. *C. acicula* is Palæarctic, spreading to the far South. *Glessula* is Oriental and in comparison limited in its area of distribution. Commencing with Southern India, it is absent from the N.W. Himalaya, bordering on the eastern margin of the Palæarctic, coming in (in Nepal?) in Sikhim and extending through the North-East Himalaya, Assam with the Assam Range, and thence to Burma, China, and Sumatra. All these are forest-clad countries with considerable rainfall, or country which was once much more forest-clad than at present, before man arrived to destroy the ancient forests. The Khasia Hills, with the Jaintia on the East, were once much more wooded than they are at present and formed a tract of country of great extent. *Geostilbia balanus*, on the other hand, may be called a desert species, standing great heat and great dryness for months. A knowledge of the animal would be of extreme value in every way. I cannot find that it has ever been seen alive.

I prefer to place *Glessula* and its subgenera in a family of its own, the Glessulidæ.

Conchologically *Glessula* possesses many very distinct characters. It comprises shells which have the columellar margin abruptly truncate at the base, which in the majority of the species forms a short gutter and holds a part of the mantle near the right dorsal margin. A well-defined division with shells of all sizes is found having elongate, turreted, and flat-sided shells, the major diameter differing little from that of the small aperture. Typical *Bacillum cassiaca* falls under the above shell description, and I shall have to refer to this subgenus—it is much more solid and opaque, with stronger regular sculpture and larger apex; the animal (December 1919) still remains to be described.

A departure from the *Bacillum* type of shell character is met with in *Glessula tenuispira* (Plate CLIX. fig. 3); the shell is thin, transparent, more or less finely striate, the aperture larger, and that and the body-whorl together are much larger than the shorter spire above.

This proportion of parts is intensified in species like Plate CLX. fig. 1 *burrailensis*, fig. 2 do., fig. 3 do., fig. 4 do., fig. 5 var. *maxwelli*; still more in fig. 9 *butleri*, fig. 11 *crassilabris*, or what may be accepted as true *Glessula*. The animal of *Glessula ochracea*, G.-A., of Sikhim, has been dissected and published in ' Records Indian Museum,' vol. viii. pt. xii. p. 617. It was found to agree with *G. orophila* as described by Semper. Until many of the smaller species are anatomically examined, they must all be placed in *Glessula*; the smallest species, such as *G. gemma*, may possibly have characters of subgeneric value.

The classification as given in ' Fauna British India,' vol. ii. (*vide* Systematic Index, p. x) requires modification. *Bacillum* is placed in the Achatinidæ subfamily *Stenogyrinæ*, whereas *Glessula* is put in the Family Ferrusacidæ Genus 3. I can find very little difference between the animals of *Glessula* and *Bacillum* (January 1920), and consider the first should come next the other in the *Stenogyrinæ*.

Conch. Ind. p. 17, "the subgenus *Bacillum* is proposed by Mr. Theobald for this (*A. obtusa*, Blf.), the preceding (*A. cassiaca*, Bs.), and other allied forms."

It was left to Mr. Henry A. Pilsbry to describe the Genus conchologically, which he does in Man. Conch. ser. 2, xviii. 1906, p. 1, as follows. He mentions 4 species and 1 subspecies.

Bacillum.—"Shell rather large, solid, imperforate, turreted, many-whorled, a little contracted near the obtuse, rounded summit; the embryonic shell cylindric; sculpture of vertical rib-striæ beginning somewhere upon the first whorl (Pl. i. fig. 12); the post-embryonic whorls being obliquely, regularly rib-striate. Aperture oblique, Achatinoid, the columellar concave, truncate at the base, outer lip simple. Internal axis slender, strongly sigmoid within each whorl. Soft anatomy unknown.

"Type, *B. cassiaenm*. Distribution, Eastern India."

The very recent and extended knowledge of the animals of *Bacillum* and *Glessula* shows that the two genera come next each other; further, that the animals of the latter present two very distinct divisions. This was first seen on dissecting a well-known species from Darjiling and Sikhim long known as *G. tennispira* in early Catalogues, such as Nevill's ' Hand-list.' The specimens dissected came from the Rishetchu, a tributary of the Teesta, and the anatomy is figured on Plate CLXV. figs. 1–1 c. On this I found a new Subgenus, with the following characters:—

Subgenus RISHETIA, nov.

Shell large, thin, transparent, imperforate, turreted, many-whorled, tapering gradually to a rather acute embryonic apex, first 2 whorls smooth ; sculpture regular, rather coarse striation. Aperture oblique, columellar concave, truncate at base.

Animal. Ovotestis tightly convoluted, close to the albumen gland. Prostate and oviduct compact cylindrical, with closely-packed follicles. Spermatheca large on long duct. Penis with a distinct simple gland or flagellum retractor muscle on side.

It is also apparent, with the gradually accumulating knowledge of the animal combined with form of the shell, the genus *Glessula* admits of subdivision—*Glessula* as a subgenus to include all those

species possessing the comb-like appendage to the penis (flagellum).
Unfortunately, up to date 1919 the animal of a true *Bacillum* has
never been obtained, never even seen alive. Still I am inclined to
think this genus comes in close to *Glessula*, in fact far closer than
does *Curvella* or *Harpalus*. The comb-like flagellum (Pl. CLXV.
fig. 2 c) is replaced by a short, pointed, simple one (Pl. CLXV.
fig. 1 a), while in a Ceylon species it is massive, with an in-
distinctly tripartite outline (Pl. CLXV. fig. 7 a, f.).

Distribution.—The absence of *Glessula* in the North-West
Himalaya and the Punjab is very remarkable, viz. from all the
old valleys of the Punjab Rivers and the Ganges. Whether this
feature extends to the Kali River and through Nepal to its eastern
boundary, the valley of the Tambur, which Sir Joseph Hooker was
the first to explore and describe, has to be discovered when that
country becomes better known and is collected in.

The only exception to the above distribution is the reported
occurrence of one species, *G. hugeli* Pfr. in Kashmir. I have never
seen or heard of its being found there; I was always collecting,
and no man in my time saw so much of Kashmir Territory
than I did. I am inclined to be sceptical, for Kashmir has been
fairly collected in by zoologists such as Stoliczka and Theobald,
who were not likely to miss finding so large and conspicuous
a shell, 37 mm. in length.

Mr. Gude says (p. 387):—"When first described, its origin
was unknown. Kashmir was first given as its habitat by Hanley
and Theobald. The species is allied to *Glessula chessoni*, but
more solid in texture. The Cuming Collection contains three
specimens from Kashmir, with a label in Pfeiffer's hand-writing."

It is, moreover, on the authority of Hanley and Theobald,
Conch. Indica, p. 33; this means "Hanley," who had little regard
for Geographical distribution. I saw a good deal of Hanley
about 1869. He never grasped the enormous size of India:
how different is the climate on its north and south, its vast
plains and mountains. Consequently I am led to think, on
learning that von Hügel had visited Kashmir, any shell connected with him Hanley assumed from that part of India.

With Eastern Nepal a great change takes place in the orography
of the Himalays; the most elevated peaks, Mt. Everest among
them, lie parallel to the plains at about 80 miles distant, and a
chain glaciated and covered with snow is continuous for 500 miles
as far as the Kali River. This must affect, even at the present day,
the temperature of the valleys draining to the plains, and surely
would have sufficed during the Glacial period to limit the Land
Mollusca to the base of the hills, from which many species would
never have returned or survived the change. It produced conditions thus far to the East similar, but on a small scale, to
the disturbance of the fauna and flora in Europe caused by
intense cold. Proceeding to the N.W. to the latitude of Kashmir,
these conditions would have been intensified, for enormous glaciers
40 miles long once filled the main valleys.

The genus ranges all over Peninsular India, is more abundant in the South, extending to Ceylon, a few species being found common on both sides. It has been studied by H. A. Pilsbry, who cites 58 species; G. K. Gude, in Faun. Brit. India, raised the number to 80; Colonel R. H. Beddome (1906) gives 53; while Nevill in his Proof Copy ' Hand-list ' (1881) records 65.

The species are very distinct; none are found outside the Peninsula, as far as my investigations go, and I have been able to correct several incorrect determinations.

The subgenus RISHETIA does not extend to South India, apparently. Beddome has recorded *R. tennispira* from North Canara, based only on a single specimen without any history: see what I say of this under the title of *longispira* No. 2, Sikhim and the Teesta valley.

Going back in time, it has not been recorded from the Inter-trappean beds of the Peninsula—those of Nagpur, for instance; but I see no reason why it should not be found in them, especially the smaller species, and it should be looked for. We do not half know the genera preserved in this old formation*. The Rev. Stephen Hislop, in the ' Proceedings ' of the Geological Society, 1859, p. 154, describes the " Tertiary Deposits associated with Trap-Rock in the East Indies," and the fossil shells are described and figured by him. Having very recently received through Dr. N. Annandale a collection of these fossils from Nagpur, I have been led to read the paper. An interesting paragraph I quote from is on p. 164 :—" I have shown my freshwater shells to Mr. Benson, the highest authority on the Molluscs of our Indian lakes, and he gives it as his opinion that not one of the specimens submitted to him exactly corresponds to anything he has seen." This was written 60 years ago; it is in accordance with my conclusions expressed in a letter to Dr. Annandale dated 31st March, 1920 : " I have had an hour's look at them, and can say they are all unknown forms to me." This rich fauna of Upper Cretaceous age should no longer lie thus neglected, for since Hislop wrote an enormous advance has been made in our knowledge and treatment of the Land and Freshwater Mollusca.

" The Zoological Results of the Abor Expedition, 1911–12," published in the ' Records Indian Museum,' vol. viii., have considerably modified our ideas of distribution and led to the records of the past (nearly forgotten) being looked up. It points to a migration of molluscan life from the far South. Perhaps no more interesting history can be recalled than my finding on Shengorh Peak, 7000 feet, in the Dafla Hills, a species I named and described as *Staffordia daflaensis*. Moll. Ind. pt. x. April 1907, p. 184, pl. cxiii. In expectation of receiving other material, I did not refer to my description of *Diakia striata*, var., from Siam, in Proc. Malacolog. Society, vol. vii. pt. 2, p. 93, pl. x. June 1906. There is no doubt

---

* In a paper on some Freshwater Fossils from Central South Africa (Annals & Mag. Nat. Hist., vol. v. March 1920) Mr. R. Bullen Newton on p. 246 refers to certain species in the Nagpur beds. Also my contribution in " Records of two Indian Museums" 1919, Oct. vol. xvi. pt. vi. on the genus Mysorella of Southern India, pointing out the necessity for their generic revision.

as to the close relationship, especially shown in the genitalia. *Diakia* did not occur among the Abor collections, unless it shall eventually turn out that *Bensonia* (?) *aborensis*, Rec. Ind. Mus. vol. viii. p. 596 (text-fig. 1), has similar anatomy. In shell character it is unlike that of any Indian Genus I have seen; but I had only one specimen to deal with.

For a knowledge of the peculiar anatomy of *Diakia*, we have to go to Semper, where he deals with what was then known as

Ariophanta rumphii	in Reisen, pl. iii.	fig. 18.
rareguttata, var. *sparsa*	" "	fig. 17.
nemorensis	" "	fig. 19.
striata, Gray = *naninoides*, Bs.	"	fig. 21 *a b*.

He gives beautiful figures of the genitalia, so unlike those of any strictly Indian Genus.

Our knowledge of the Assam Land Mollusca is very imperfect; much has still to be done, with small chance of our knowing more under present conditions. In fact, discovery of species of great interest is sheer luck; unless the conditions are exceedingly good, perfect in fact, nothing is found. To exemplify this, I will give an experience of my own when in the Dafla Hills.

Shengorh Peak was one of my Trigonometrical Stations, and I had to clear the forest before I could commence observations. Rain set in soon after pitching camp; so I had plenty of leisure to collect in Natural History. The wet brought out the shells and slug-like forms, and I had a busy time making drawings and taking notes of colour and size. I secured what in drier weather I should never have got, certainly not alive; among them was this unique Genus *Staffordia*, whose nearest relative known to us is found at Chantaboon in Siam. It doubtless occurs at many intermediate places which have yet to be discovered, when its possible ancient connection with Assam may be explained.

This is the history of a visit to one high point, one which over-looked the great broad valley of the Subansiri, extending far back to the base of the snowy range, away to hundreds of peaks covered with primeval forest. The imagination fails to picture what the result of exploration would be, combined with knowledge of how and what to collect. In these solitudes Nature reigns supreme; one does not often find such a spot seldom visited by man, never lived in by him.

The birds on this Peak were fearless. I was quite struck by the behaviour of a beautiful little *Suthora*, which kept hovering about my head and would perch on a twig a yard from my face.

Starting with Sikhim and the valley of the Teesta, where species are numerous, I take in succession going eastward the great valleys of the Eastern Himalaya to the Brahmaputra, they go far back in geological time—are older, in fact, than the Sivaliks, for down their courses all the waste of the Himalaya has passed either to the sea, as in the case of the Teesta, or to build up the above formation. The vast thickness of these Tertiary rocks, originally deposited not far above sea-level, the basement beds being even marine, as near Samaguting, is well seen on the Assam Range south of the Brahmaputra, where they are elevated to 10,000 feet in the Patkai and Naga Hills. In the Garo Hills this dimishes to 3000 feet, but they are there in force with a thickness of some 5000–6000 feet: *vide* 'Journal Asiatic Society of Bengal,' vol. xxxviii. pt. 2, no. 1, 1869, with a Geological Map of a portion of the Khasi Hills near longitude 91° E.

Connected with this range of the genus, two facts stand out:— (1) The extreme age of the great valleys; (2) the great difference between the Molluscan fauna of Sikhim and that of the Datla Hills, still more when it is compared with that of the Arbor country. There are very few species common to both. Few Sikhim species are found in either: all is new, even new genera come in. The reason for this is no doubt due to the physical features of the great valleys: some, such as the Monass and Subansiri, are very broad; they go back far into the Range; their sources glacial, they are separated one from the other by lofty snow-covered longitudinal ranges, which continue high to the plains. They are thus completely isolated one from the other, allowing evolution to go on independently within them and form "specific centres."

The rich flora and fauna of Sikhim is in direct relationship to its position at the head of the Bay of Bengal, and for ages has received accessions from that, the Southern side; so with species of *Glessula*, when those at present living between the Teesta and the Monass are compared with those of the Khasi and Garo Hills, 100 miles to the south, how small and yet how defined is the difference.

Himalaya area:	Represented in the Khasi-Garo area:
longispira.	*tenuispira.*
hastula.	*subhastula.*
baculina.	*sub-baculina.*

Between these two areas there is an indication of a once more continuous land-surface higher that at present. All this delta area has gone through considerable depression with denudation. This is so well exemplified by the isolated, weathered masses of intrusive granite rising abruptly out of the alluvium by which they are surrounded at Chanda Dinga, opposite Gwalpara and Doobri. My Survey work took me to the top of several such hills. Granite intrusion is frequently seen; it is to be noted at Tura and Riwnk on the Assam Range, and similar intrusions occur further east and north intimately connected with the forces of upheaval. Those near Gwalpara, on the north side of the Brahmaputra, no doubt originally passed up and through stratified rocks long since denuded (perhaps of Cretaceous age) which cover so large an area in the Garo Hills, where they have also suffered great denudation.

Numbers, followed by the letters B.M., refer to specimens catalogued in three collections presented to the British Museum, viz. those of 1. W. T. Blanford and H. F. Blanford combined, 2. Colonel H. Beddome, 3. Godwin-Austen; they cannot fail to assist those who may study this group or have to name specimens from India.

1. *North-West Himalaya.* (No species as yet found).

DISTRIBUTION OF THE GENUS *GLESSULA* IN THE GANGETIC DELTA,
NORTH EAST FRONTIER OF INDIA, AND BURMA.

2. *Sikhim and the Teesta Valley, with Western Bhutan,
including the Delta.*

Long. 88° to 89° East.

Glessula (Rishetia) longispira, n. sp.	{ Pl. CLIX. figs. 1, 2. { Pl. CLIV. figs. 1-1 c.
baculina, Henry Blanford.	Pl. CLIX. fig. 7.
var. *exilis*.	Pl. CLIX. figs. 13, 14.
rissomensis, n. sp.	Pl. CLIX. fig. 6.
hastula, Benson.	{ Pl. CLIX. figs. 16, 17. { Pl. CLXIII. figs. 9, 9 a.
roberti. n. sp.	Pl. CLXIII. fig. 10.
rarhiensis, n. sp.	Pl. CLXII. fig. 23.
Glessula ochracea, Godwin-Austen.	Pl. CLX. fig. 8.
orobia, Benson.	Pl. CLXII. figs. 5, 6.
var. *major*.	Pl. CLXII. fig. 7.
small var.	Pl. CLXII. fig. 9.
crassula, Reeve.	{ Pl. CLXII. fig. 24. { Pl. CLXIV. figs. 14, 15.

From the Delta.

Glessula sarrissa, Bs.	Pl. CLXI. fig. 10.
gemma, Bs.	Pl. CLXI. figs. 26, 27, 28, 29.
var. *minuta*, G.-A.	

GLESSULA (RISHETIA) LONGISPIRA, n. sp. (Plate CLIX. figs. 1, 2,
shells; Plate CLXV. figs. 1-1 c, anatomy.) No. 552 B.M.

Locality. Risett Chu, Sikhim (*Wm. Robert*).

Shell elongately turreted; sculpture: fine, regular and rather
coarse striation; colour ruddy ochraceous; spire very long, sides
straight, apex attenuate: suture shallow; whorls 13, sides flat,
proportion of length to last whorl 100 : 34; aperture small, oval;
peristome thin; columellar margin slightly convex.

Size: maj. diam. 9·5; length 44 mm.

In the Blanford collection (No. 238.06.2.2) one specimen measured
47·5 mm. in length, and is the largest I have seen.

Shell of animal dissected 40 × 9½ mm.; whorls 13 (No. 552
B.M.).

The generative organs (Pl. CLXV. figs. 1 a, 1 b).—These are
naturally very elongate and twisted; the hermaphrodite duct is
long and closely coiled. The albumen gland elongately oval, uterus
and oviduct very long, compact, cylindrical, the oviduct showing
broad, close convolutions (follicles). The penis is a simple sheath,

with the vas deferens given off at the extreme distal end, close to the gland (*f*) which represents the flagellum. In the second specimen dissected this is well shown (fig. 1 *b*); it is small, short, slightly hooked, not flat and notched as in *G. ochracea*. Further on, in a species from Cachar, a small variety of *G. garoense* (turreted and elongate) a similar short flagellum was found (Plate CLXV. fig. 6). The spermatheca (*sp.*) is an elongate sac on a long stalk. The retractor muscle is given off about half-way down the side of the sheath.

The animal (fig. 1) can withdraw into the shell as far back as the three last whorls. The sole of the foot is widely segmented from side to side. Contracted in spirits the animal has about 8 whorls (fig. 1 *c*). There are narrow right and left dorsal lobes, and on the columellar side a muscular cylindrical mass fills the characteristic groove.

GLESSULA LONGISPIRA, n. sp.   (Plate CLIX. fig. 2.)

Locality. Rarhichu, Sikhim (*W. Robert*).   No. 3593 B.M.
Animal. Foot short, rich grey black, surface minutely papillate, in strong contrast with the sole, which is pale ochraceous, narrowly segmented transversely.

Length to last whorl 100 : 39.

The jaw is slightly convex, very thin and transparent, and under high power is seen to be made up of very numerous narrow elongate plates.

Size : length 37 ; maj. diam. 8·75 mm.

From the Rechila Peak on Sikhim border and Western Bhutan, Mr. Wm. Robert sent me five specimens (No. 28 B.M.), sepia-brown in colour, and with far stronger sculpture, which may be considered a local variety. The largest has 12 whorls, and measures 37·75 × 9·25 mm.

Anatomical investigation shows that there are two very distinct sections of *Glessula*, and so far they conform to shell character—for how great conchologically is the difference between the turreted very long species and the glossy, oblong-conoid forms ? The short oblong species, such as *G. gamma*, have yet to be examined—they may have some character of their own, viewed anatomically.

In this genus and this particular species it may be said I am laying considerable, even undue stress, on variation in a single organ—the penis —and of that only a part. This will be noted and felt even more by conchologists, some explanation therefore seems necessary for entering into physiological details. The flagellum is a very small organ, but one of great importance ; in the developmental life of the animal it has a most important part to play. Within it is formed the spermatophore, which is filled with spermatozoon, and eventually, in the act of copulation, is transferred to the spermatheca of the other individual—its spines keep it in position on its passage and retain it there. In different genera, it takes on more or less very complicated forms and becomes a very important character, often far more easily described than the shell itself. In the South African genera, *Peltatus* and *Kerkophorus,* it is a beautiful object in the microscope.

Under *Glessula tenuispira,* Benson. Colonel Beddome in his notes on Indian and Ceylonese species of *Glessula* in the ' Proceedings of the Malacological Society of London,' vol. vii., Sept. 1906, p. 160, says : " Full grown ones collected in the Teesta Valley near Darjiling and in North Canara measure 44 mm. in length (*vide* Plate CLIX. fig. 1) and have fourteen whorls." The single example recorded from N. Canara is now in the Natural History Museum and is before me. This is a part of India which was well known to Colonel Beddome—in fact, where his work as head of the Forest Department lay. It is noticeable there should be no history, no remark on the very remarkable occurrence of this species in Southern India, and that only a single specimen was secured. Until it is rediscovered very considerable doubt must attach to the accuracy of the habitat. The specimen may even have been purchased.

GLESSULA CANARAENSIS, n. sp. (Plate CLIX. fig. 8.) No. 681 Bedd. Coll. B.M.

Locality. N. Canara, collector unknown. (A single specimen, if found again.)

Shell elongately turreted ; sculpture : irregular fine striation ; colour pale ochraceous ; spire long, apex rather blunt, rounded : suture impressed, very slightly notched on lower margin by the striation ; whorls 14, flatly convex ; aperture oblique, ovate ; columellar margin slightly concave, truncate below.

Size : maj. diam. 8·5 : length 41·25 mm.

After very careful comparison with all the specimens in the Blanford and my own collection, I believe this to be a fine, more attenuate example of *G. longispira,* and that it really came from the neighbourhood of Darjiling. It is a single specimen, and its presence in Southern India has to be confirmed and the animal examined.

GLESSULA BACULINA, H. F. Blanford, No. 9–9.iii.15 B.M. (Plate CLIX. fig. 7.)

J. A. S. B. xl. 1871, p. 43, pl. ii. fig. 6.

Original description :—" *Testa elongato-turrita, gracilis, tenuis-cula, oblique striata, fusco vel fulvo cornea, epidermide nitescente induta. Spira turrita, apice obtusull. Anfractus 13, parum convexi; inferiores subaequales; sutura impressa, minute denticulata. Apertura obliqua, ovato-triangularis ; peristoma simplex, actum. Columella abrupte arcuata, oblique producta, ad basin verticaliter truncata.*

" Alt. 38 mm. ; diam. 6·5–7·5 mm. ; aperturæ alt. 7, lat. 4 mm.

" Cepit Dr. F. Stoliczka apud Kherstong Himalayæ Sikkimensis.

" This species appears to have escaped the notice of all previous collectors in Sikkim ; it was found in association with its near ally *G. tenuispira*, Bens., by Dr. Stoliczka during a recent visit. It is easily distinguished from the latter species by its slenderness (the diameter being ⅛ of the length), and the comparative narrowness of its whorls ; moreover, by the form of the columella, the lower part of which is bent abruptly almost at right angles with the slope of the inner lip : while in *G. tenuispira*, *G. erosa*, and other allied forms, the curvature is at the utmost obtuse. Specimens, the shell of which had been slightly weathered, show fine spiral markings, but these are not visible unless the shell has become somewhat opaque. The animal is dark leaden grey, somewhat paler at the sides of the foot.

" The following is a list of the species now known from Sikhim :— *G. tenuispira*, Bens., *G. crassula*, Bens., *G. hastula*, Bens., *G. orobia*, Bens., *G. erosa*, nob., *G. baculina*, nob."

When going through Henry Blanford's collection, bequeathed to the British Museum by his brother, I came on the type specimens of the above species ; these I had not seen for 40 years. At the time I was staying with him in Calcutta, he placed them in my hands to figure for a paper he was preparing for the Asiatic Society of Bengal, vol. xl. pt. 2, 1871, p. 39. It is a very distinct species. I have quite a large series obtained since from different localities in Sikhim and Western Bhutan. Beddome (Pro. Malacol. Soc. 1906), in his paper on the genus, considers it only a more slender form of *G. tenuispira*, Bs., a view most difficult to fall in with and support. There is a very considerable difference in general form— that is, when compared with the so-called *tenuispira* of Sikhim. Mr. Gude credits me with having found it in the Khasi Hills (F. B. Ind. ii. p. 379), probably on the authority of Geoffrey Nevill, in his Hand-list, p. 170. The Khasi form is quite distinct and described further on.

In the Beddome collection put up in the same box are four shells under this name, with two labels in Beddome's handwriting. One has on it (three in pencil) " Darjiling, H. F. Bl.," the other (one in pencil) " Thyet Myo." It is easy to see the difference in this last from the others, the apex is much more attenuate, the aperture larger and broader. The Darjiling shells are quite typical, and I have compared them with Henry Blanford's types.

G. baculina was found by Mr. Wm. Robert at Zemo Samdong in Sikhim, some 60 miles up the Sikhim Valley—there smaller, 28 × 6·25 mm. (No. 553 B.M.)

GLESSULA (RISHETIA) BACULINA, H. Blf. var. *exilis*. (Plate CLIX. figs. 13, 14.)

Locality. Rissom Peak, Sikhim (3595 B.M.)—Type. Damsang, Sikhim (3594) (*W. Robert*).

Shell elongately turreted ; sculpture : rather close raised striation, oblique ; colour umber-brown ; spire long, apex fine,

first three whorls nearly same diameter ; suture impressed : whorls
12, flatly convex, body whorl and aperture ⅜ of total length ;
aperture ovate, small : peristome thin ; columella sharply curved,
truncate.

Size (Damsang) : maj. diam. 5·5 ; length 24·75 mm.

(Rissom) :   ,,   5·7   ,,   30·00   ,,

This is close to *G. baculina*, but the whorls are not so flat as in
that species, and it is very much smaller.

GLESSULA (RISHETIA) RISSOMENSIS, n. sp.   (Plate CLIX. fig. 6
of a Damsang shell.)   No. 3570 B.M.

Locality. Rissom Peak and Damsang, east of the Teesta Valley
(*W. Robert*).

Shell elongately turreted ; sculpture : close irregular striation
well marked ; colour dull white with a pale ochre tint ; spire :
apex blunt and rounded, sides nearly straight ; suture impressed :
whorls 10, the embryonic large and rounded smooth, sides flatly
convex ; aperture ovate ; outer lip with a good deal of convexity ;
columellar margin very slightly convex.

Size (Rissom Peak) : maj. diam. 6·25 ; alt. axis 24·5 mm.

I have this preserved in spirit : the animal is pale coloured
throughout. The specimens are not fully grown, the larger apex
distinguishes it at once from *G. baculina.* It approaches
G. harmuttiensis of the Dafla Hills, but the apex of that shell is
finer, the embryonic whorls being closer together. Specimens
were also obtained on Rissom Peak.

GLESSULA (RISHETIA) HASTULA, Benson. (880.06.1.1.) (Plate CLXI.
fig. 16) ; (No. 16.9.iii.15 B.M.) (Plate CLXI. fig. 17) ; (for apex
enlarged, Plate CLXIII. figs. 9, 9 a, 10.)

Achatina hastula, Benson, A. M. N. H. ser. 3, vol. 5 (1860) p. 461.

Original description :—" *Testa turrito-subulata, tenui, oblique
capilluceo-striata, fusco-cornea, nitidula ; spira subulata, apice obtuso,
sutura profundiuscula ; anfractibus 9. primis convexis, postremis
convexiusculis, ultimo ⅔ testæ attingente ; apertura vix obliqua,
ovato-elliptica, peristomatis marginibus callo, tenui junctis, dextrali
recto acuto columellari arcuato calloso albido, basi oblique truncata.*

" Long. 12¼, diam. 3½ mill. ; long. apert. 3¼ mill.

" Habitat ad Pankabari, prope Darjiling, raro. Teste W. T.
Blanf.

" Of a more slender form than the large *Ach. tenuispira,* B., the
whorls increasing very gradually, and not attenuate towards
the upper part of the spire as in that species."

This species was originally found by W. T. Blanford at Punkabari
at the foot of the Darjiling Hills.

It has been recorded by Theobald and Stoliczka as occurring in
Burma, Kumah Hill and Maii, Sandway District, Arakan (repeated

by Gude in Fauna B. India, vol. ii. p. 414). In a paper by them in the Journal of the Asiatic Society of Bengal (vol. xli. 1872, p. 341) they say: "somewhat larger than the Sikhimtype shell." This record is of little value, when one considers how cursorily some shells, particularly of *Glessula*, have been looked at and how little time is often bestowed upon them. Nevill in his Hand-list, p. 169, only gives the Darjiling locality. Theobald, it would appear, never gave specimens to the Calcutta Museum, and it is impossible to say where these shells of his went to.

In W. T. Blanford's collection is a single typical specimen (No. 880.06.1.1), and on a label in Hanley's handwriting a note " Identical with the large one figured in the Conch. Indica " (Plate XVIII. fig. 4). Two specimens were in the Henry Blanford collection which may be considered also typical, as the two brothers were constantly exchanging specimens.

I find *Glessula hastula*, Bs., does not extend to the Garo and Khasi Hill ranges, its place being taken by a shell at first sight very similar to it, but which on close examination is found to differ sufficiently to describe, making it all the more improbable that *G. hastula* extends to Arakan. *G. hastula* of Darjiling is more attenuate with more costulate sculpture than in the Khasi form.

Apex enlarged of (880.06.1.1 B.M.) Plate CLXIII. figs. 9, 9 a, Darjiling, and of (557 B.M.) fig. 10, Richila.

It may be noted that the apex of the last differs very much from that of a typical *hastula*, a good character and sufficient to create a species which I name after Mr. W. Robert, late of the Indian Survey, who made for me such a splendid collection when he was working in Sikhim. There are only two specimens and one other from Rissom Peak (No. 2483 B.M.). It is very possible other examples will be found among my spirit-specimens.

GLESSULA (RISHETIA) ROBERTI, n. sp.

Locality. Richila Peak, Western Bhutan (No. 557 B.M.)—Type. Rissom Peak, Sikhim (No. 2483 B.M.) (*W. Robert*).

Shell subulately turreted ; sculpture : very regular, close well-raised striation, commencing on apex (Plate CLXIII. fig. 10) ; colour chestnut-brown ; spire elongate, side flattened, apex blunt, rounded ; suture slightly impressed ; whorls 8½, very regularly increasing, sides flatly convex ; aperture small, ovate ; columellar margin concave.

Size : maj. diam. 3·5 ; alt. axis 11 mm.

GLESSULA RARHIENSIS, n. sp. (Plate CLXII. fig. 23.)

Locality. Rarhichu Valley, Sikhim (10 specimens) (No. 3335 B.M.) (*W. Robert*).

Shell elongately conical, shiny ; sculpture : distant irregular striæ ; colour dark umber-brown ; spire high, sides flattish, apex blunt : suture impressed ; whorls 8, flatly convex, rather regular

18 LAND AND FRESHWATER

in size, i.e., increasing very gradually; aperture narrowly oval; columellar margin very slightly convex.

Size: maj. diam. 4·0; alt. axis 11·20 mm.

This is more elongate than *G. crassula*, but similar in coloration and sculpture. It is certainly more than a variety of the Darjiling shell.

In Wm. Blanford's collection is a single specimen, which I refer to this species, found by him on the Chola range at 11,000 ft.

GLESSULA OCHRACEA, Godwin-Austen. (Plate CLX. fig. 8.)

Records Indian Museum. vol. viii. pt. xii. p. 617, 1918, fig. ix. A.B.C. (genitalia).

Locality. Rarhiclm, Sikhim. Type. (No. 3592 B.M.) Richila Peak, var. (No. 555 B.M.) (*W. Robert*).

Shell conically turreted and elongate, solid, smooth, and shining: sculpture: very regular sharp striation: colour dark rich ochre. a paler margin to the peristome: spire high, sides slightly convex, apex blunt; suture impressed; whorls 7½, flatly convex, the last tumid; aperture oval; peristome well thickened; columellar margin strong, curved, notch at base deep.

Size: maj. diam. 9·25; length 21·25 mm.

Animal (Plate CLXV. fig. 2 A). With short foot, the sole of which has a central groove each side closely segmented.

The buccal mass (Plate CLXV. fig. 2 B) is globose and small with a very strong retractor muscle; the salivary gland is in a single bilobed mass, one side long and pointed.

In the generative organs (Plate CLXV. fig. 2 c) the hermaphrodite duct is conspicuous by its size, is very long and strongly and closely convoluted. The albumen gland is very globose. The uterus and closely convoluted oviduct short. The penis is a folded sheath, and what I take to represent the flagellum is a flattened mass, straight on one side, having a serrate edge on the other, consisting of a short terminal and ten longer notches, very characteristic and unusual in form. A similar flagellum is met with in *orophila*, Bs., as figured by Professor Semper (Reis. Archipel. 1873, p. 133, Taf. xii. figs. 14–16, under *Cionella*) there is one terminal and 30 notches, giving it a feather-like form. The vas deferens joins the penis close to this at the distal end.

The spermatheca is oblong, rather short, on a short thick base.

GLESSULA OCHRACEA, G.-A., var.

Locality. Richila Peak (*W. Robert*).
Is larger and a much darker ochre than the type.
Maj. diam. 10; length 24·25 mm.

Glessula orobia, Bs. (No. 17.9.iii.15 B.M.) (Plate CLXII. figs. 5, 6; Plate CLXIII. fig. 4, apex of No. 17; Plate CLXV. figs. 4-4 *b*, genitalia).

Achatina orobia, B. A. M. N. H. ser. 3, v. p. 461 (1880).

Locality. Senchal and Darjiling.

Original description :—" *Testa ovata-oblonga, solidiuscula, lævigata, leviter striata, striis non-nullis remotiusculis profunde impressis sculpta, nitida, olivaceo-cornea; spira convexo pyramidata, apice obtuso, sutura impressa; anfractibus 6½-7½ convexiusculis, ad humerum angulatis, crenulatis, ultimo ⅓ testæ superante; apertura verticali semiovali, columella valde arcuata, callosa, basi oblique truncata, peristomate recto, crassiusculo, obtuso.*

" Long. 11, diam. 5 mill.; apert. 4 mill. longa, 3 lata.

" Habitat ad Sinchul et Darjiling (alt. ped. 8500 et 7000). Teste W. T. Blanford.

" Distinguished from the larger Khasia species, *A. crassilabris*, B., by its peculiar sculpture, and by the formation of the whorls below the suture."

The specimen figured is from Hy. Blanford's collection No. 17, 9.iii.15, and measures 11·25 × 5 mm. There are two other examples, and in another box (No. 243, 06.2.2 B.M.) are four others all alike and from Darjiling.

Mr. Gude, in ' Fauna British India, Mollusca,' ii. 1914, says : " Some specimens in the Beddome collection from the Naga Hills, composed of 6½ whorls, measure 8 × 3·5 mm., and refers to another shell also from the same locality, possessing only six whorls, with rather convex sides, measuring 6·5 × 3 mm." I have now seen these (No. 768 of my catalogue of the shells selected out of the Beddome collection). They are *Glessula prowiensis*, mihi, and very different in every way. The apex of one is given on Plate CLXIII. fig. 4; also that of *G. orobia* from the Henry Blanford collection, No. 17, fig. 8.

Glessula orobia, Bs., var. MAJOR. (Plate CLXII. fig. 7.)

Richila Peak, Sikhim. Type. (No. 556 B M.)
Damsang, Sikhim. (No. 3336.)

This is a much larger shell, yet has all the characters of the Darjiling examples in its general form and increase of the whorls. It is, however, a dark umber-brown, and in this respect is like *crassula* from the same peak, which is a much smaller shell.

Var. *major* measures : maj. diam. 5·2 ; length 13·0 mm.

Glessula orobia, var. MAJOR. (No. 556 B.M.) Damsang, Sikhim. (Plate CLXV. fig. 4.)

The generative organs were seen complete and proved of great interest. The appendage given off near the junction of the vas deferens at head of the penis is small and hand-shaped ; it consists

c 2

of finger-like lobes, one short, and three united together longer (figs. 4 a and 4 b). It represents in a shorter form the same appendage in *G. ochracea*, in which there is one short and ten comb-like notches, and the still longer one as represented by Semper in *G. orophila*, which has led to its being described as a feather-like gland and typical of the genus; a better knowledge of the animals shows it will only apply to a section of the genus. The elongate forms certainly form another, and may possibly have to be included in *Bacillum*.

The prostate (fig. 4) is round, short, and solid; the hermaphrodite duct, much convoluted and thickened, forming a mass close to the albumen gland. The teeth of the radula do not differ from those of other species dissected. The formula is

$$16 \cdot 9 \cdot 1 \cdot 9 \cdot 16$$
$$\text{or} \qquad 25 \cdot 1 \cdot 25.$$

GLESSULA OROBIA, Bs., small var. (Plate CLXII. fig. 9.)

Locality. Richila Peak, Western District. (No. 558 B.M.) (*W. Robert*).

Shell elongately conical, shining, somewhat tumid; sculpture: irregular distant striation; colour umber-brown with a greenish tint; spire rather short; suture impressed; whorls $6\frac{1}{2}$; columellar margin slightly curved, truncate at base.

Size: figured shell, maj. diam. 3·75; alt. axis 8·0 mm.
  largest   „   4·0   „   9·0 „

GLESSULA CRASSULA, Reeve, Bs. MS. (Plate CLXII. fig. 24.)

Locality. Darjiling No. 18.9.iii.15, B.M. Typical from Hy. Blanford's collection.

Shell elongately conical, smooth and shining, slender; sculpture: very few and distant striæ; colour umber-brown; whorls $6\frac{1}{2}$.

Size: maj. diam. 3·0: alt. axis. 7·5 mm.
  largest   „   8·0 „
These are all small and shorter than dimensions given in the original description, viz., 9 mm.

In the Beddome collection are three specimens (No. 753) from the Naga Hills which bear a label in Col. Beddome's handwriting, *G. crassula.* I have compared them carefully and drawn the apex (Plate CLXIV. fig. 18) much enlarged; it differs altogether in the sculpture from typical Darjiling examples of *crassula* (Plate CLXIV. fig. 14) in the Blanford collection (No. 18) (Plate CLXIV. fig. 15). No. 753 is *G. barakensis.*

From the Rarhichu in Sikhim I have 7 examples (No. 2481), which I consider a variety of the Darjiling form. The whorls have flatter sides, and the apex is much more blunt (Plate CLXIV. fig. 15). The largest measures a little over 9 mm. in length.

In the 'Fauna of British India, Mollusca,' vol. ii. p. 429, under

this species, " Khasi, Dafla and Naga Hills" is given as the range
of this species and as collected by me. I hope soon to see these
examples, not having found them in my own collection. The
identification is Geoffrey Nevill's. I do not think he looked
sufficiently closely at them. Mr. Gude has simply copied from
Nevill's ' Hand-list,' p. 169, " 30 specimens." These I trust are
not now all mixed together. Jaintia Hills (Beddome) is also
given on p. 429. These I have seen, they are No. 751 of my
catalogue (5 examples). They are not *crassula*, but a small var.
of *crassilabris*.

GLESSULA SUBJERDONI, Beddome, Nevill MS.

Under this title the species is recorded by Geoffrey Nevill in his
amended copy of the ' Hand-list' facing page 167. Four specimens
from the Jeypur Hills, Madras, received from Col. R. H. Beddome.
Nevill gives the measurement as: long. 9, diam. 3¾ mm. ; anfr. 7.
This would be the var. *minor* of Beddome.

In the ' Fauna British India, Mollusca,' 1914, p. 434, Mr. Gude
gives Darjiling as a habitat of this species from specimens he had
found in the Beddome collection. These are No. 814 of my catalogue
of that collection : the name *subjerdoni* had been written by Beddome in pencil, a sign he had not determined it to his satisfaction ;
nor had I, when I came across it first in 1912, when under the
direction of the British Museum authorities I commenced working
at the shells in the Beddome collection and making a catalogue of
them. In August 1914, when duty in the country prevented my
going as usual to town, Mr. Gude obtained access to the Beddome
collection of *Glessula* through those who had charge of it—very
improperly, I consider, when it had been placed in my charge and a
catalogue was in progress. Thus Mr. Gude was working at this
collection, quite unknown to me, for a considerable time—some
three months,—and when seen again by me was in a new state of
arrangement, as put on record in my catalogue.

In the interests of the distribution of Indian species it would
not be fair treatment to overlook such record. I have, therefore,
gone carefully over all the specimens of *subjerdoni* in the Beddome
collection, so as to arrive at some better knowledge of them. I
have had photographs made of the shells and made myself enlarged
drawings with camera lucida of the apical whorls of the following
three specimens, a better means of showing differences than any
description :—

No. 812. Bedd. coll. *G. subjerdoni*, Bedd., Golconda Hills.
(Plate CLXIV. apex fig. 7.)
No. 809. Bedd. coll. *G. subjerdoni*, Bedd., Tennevelly Valley.
(Plate CLXIV. apex fig. 6.)
No. 811. Bedd. coll. *G. subjerdoni*, var. *minor*. Typical Jeypur
Hills. (Plate CLXIV. apex fig. 5.)

By this test the so-called *G. subjerdoni* of Darjiling (No. 814 of the Beddome collection) (Plate CLXIV. fig. 13) does not agree with the species from the typical locality, the Golconda Hills. It is, in my opinion, a large variety of *Glessula crassula*, Bs.

GLESSULA SARISSA, Benson. (No. 1596 B.M.) (Plate CLXI. fig. 10.)

Faguirabanda, Jessore, Lower Bengal (*Godwin - Austen*) (270.06.2.2) Diamond Harbour, Hoogly River (*W. T. Blanford*). Size : maj. diam. 6·8 ; length 18·8 mm. This is a finer specimen than the type described by Benson by nearly 3 mm. I give enlarged figure of the apex (Plate CLXIII. fig. 18).

Achatina sarissa, B. A. M. N. H. ser. 3, vol. v. p. 463 (1860). Original description :—" *Testa elongato-conica, tenui, lævigata, striatula, anfractibus ultimis sub lente confertim obsolete decussatis, nitidissima, olivacceo-cornea ; spira elongato-pyramidata, apice obtuso, sutura impressa ; anfractibus 7½ convexiusculis, ultimo ⅖ testæ superante ; apertura subverticali, ovato-elliptica, columella obliqua, leviter arcuata, albido-callosa, basi oblique truncata, peristomate recto, tenui.*
" Long. 16, diam. 5½ mill. ; apert. 5 mill. longa, 3½ lata.'
" Habitat prope Comereolly, Bengaliæ, ad ripas flaminis Gangis— Detexit Dr. Theodore Cantor."

GLESSULA GEMMA, Bs.; Reeve, Conch. Icon. Achatina, pl. 22. f. 123.

Original description :—" *Testa ovato-oblonga, solidiuscula, lævigata, nitida, pellucida, purpurascenti-cornea ; spira elato-conica, apice acutiuscula ; sutura profunda : anfr. 6 convexiusculi ; ultimus ⅖ longitudinis æquans, basi rotundatus ; columella arcuata, subcallosa, parist. simplex, rectum, margine dextro et basali leviter arquatis.*
" Long. 8–8½, diam. 4 mill., ap. 3 mill., longa 2 lata."

As a subgenus of *Cionella* it was made the type by Von Martens. No. 3559. From Khoostia, Bengal. (Plate CLXI. fig. 26.)
4. Hy. Blf. (9.iii.15). From Bengal; authentic sp. (Plate CLXI. fig. 27.)
No. 3382. From Chandanagore. (Plate CLXI. fig. 28.) Received from Nevill.
5. Hy. Blf. (9.iii.15). From Chittagong, var. (Plate CLXI. fig. 29.)
No. 3391. From Garo Hills. I have two specimens, much smaller and less tumid than the typical shell, measuring 6 × 3 mm. Six whorls. This I distinguish as var. *minuta*. It is dark umber in colour.
This species is thus spread over the whole front of the Delta of the Ganges and Brahmaputra.

3. The Dafla Hills,

with the Plain of the Brahmaputra on south.

Glessula (Rishetia) harmuttiensis, n. sp.	Pl. CLXX. fig. 5.
sarissa, Bs., var.	Pl. CLXI. fig. 8.
sarissa, Bs., var.	Pl. CLXIII. figs. 16, 17, 19.
subhebis, Nevill MS., n. sp.	{ Pl. CLXI. fig. 6. Pl. CLXIV. fig. 1.
nevilliana, n. sp.	{ Pl. CLXI. fig. 11. Pl. CLXI. figs. 12, 13. Pl. CLXIV. fig. 3.
dikrangense, n. sp.	Pl. CLX. figs. 7. 7 *a*.
(Dikrangia) nevilli, G.-A.	
Glessula crassilabris, Bs. var.	Pl. CLXIV. fig. 17.

See on, under this species—Khasi Hills.

GLESSULA (RISHETIA) HARMUTTIENSIS, n. sp. (Plate CLIX. fig. 5.)

Locality.—Harmutti, base of Dafla Hills, No. 445 B.M. (*Godwin-Austen*).

Shell elongately turreted; sculpture quite smooth to the naked eye, but under magnification distant obscure striation is seen; colour pale ochre to dull umber-brown; spire very long, sides flat, apex blunt; suture impressed; whorls 12, sides flat; aperture oval; peristome outer lip thin; columellar margin curving evenly.

Size: maj. diam. 7·0; alt. axis 31·9 mm.

This takes the place in the Dafla Hills of *G. baculina* of Sikhim. It is very similar in all respects, but the apex is more obtuse and the sculpture is very different: there are four specimens.

Two young specimens, unnamed, were found in Henry Blanford's collection, given to him by me.

GLESSULA (RISHETIA?) SARISSA, Bs. var. No. 445 B.M.

Locality. Burroi Gorge, Dafla Hills, four specimens (*Godwin-Austen*).

Shell elongately conical, smooth, and glossy; sculpture variable, rather regular fine striation, in some it is less and more distant; colour very pale ochraceous; spires elongate, sides slightly convex, apex finer than in the type (Pl. CLXIII. fig. 16); suture impressed; whorls 9½, sides flatly convex; aperture ovate; peristome thin; columellar margin sharply concave.

Size: maj. diam. 7·0; length 20·0 mm.

Fakirabanda, Jessore (typical spec.) } maj. diam. 6·8; length 18·8 mm.

Moisraka Ghat, Bengal, do. „ 7·5; „ 21·5 „

The figure in the 'Conchologia Indica,' pl. xxxvii. fig. 2, is a very good one, and undoubtedly of Benson's species.

The Blanford collection (No. 844, 06.1.1, B.M.) contained 3 specimens from the Dafla Hills, sent to him by me, but probably not the same locality. They are about the same size, and had been labelled (*G. tennispora?* by Blanford, but they are not like the Teria Ghat examples with which I have compared them.

GLESSULA (RISHETIA?) SARISSA, Bs., var.   No. 3566 B.M.

Locality. Barowli Gorge, Durrang District, Assam (*Godwin-Austen*).

Shell as in last; sculpture indistinct, fine longitudinal ribs follow below the suture; colour pale dull ochraceous, two closely parallel whitish bands below the suture; suture impressed; whorls 8, regularly increasing; columellar margin concave.

Size: maj. diam. 6·0; length 16·25 mm.

Only a single specimen.

GLESSULA (RISHETIA?) SARISSA, Bs., var.

From Koliaghur, Granite Tila, near Tezpur, on the left bank of the Brahmaputra, a single specimen very close to this species was found by me; smooth, with little sculpture. No. 3568 B.M. (Plate CLXI. fig. 8.)

Apex (Pl. CLXIII. fig. 19).

From Gowhathi (No. 3383 B.M.), two specimens, the apex is yet more acuminate (*vide* Pl. CLXIII. fig. 17), but there is little difference to be noted in the general shape.

GLESSULA SUBHEBES, Nevill MS., n. sp. (Plate CLXI. fig. 6; Plate CLXIV. apex, fig. 1.)

Locality. Pichola nulla, Dalla Hills. No. 1618 B.M. Type. Five examples (*Godwin-Austen*). No. 3341 B.M., Dalla, typical.

Shell oblong turreted, thin, smooth, glassy; sculpture: rather distant and fine striation, slight tendency to crenulation at suture; colour very pale ochraceous; spire long, sides slightly convex, apex blunt, 3 first whorls nearly equal; suture impressed; whorls 10, with well-marked flat convexity; aperture narrowly ovate; columella with a very slight curve downward.

Size: maj. diam. 5·0; length 15·75 mm.

From the eggs in tube containing shells it is oviparous.

This species is entered by Nevill in the interleaved copy (facing p. 167) he left to me shortly before his death, from the above locality. He gives the dimensions of a specimen in the Indian Museum which he received from me: " 15½ × 5 mm., anfr. 9."

It is the *Achatina (Glessula) hebes* in my paper on the Helicidæ of the Dalla Hills (Jour. Asiat. Soc. Bengal, vol. xlv. pt. 2, 1876, p. 315), and was a common shell.

Very fortunately I have received from the Indian Museum, for which I have to thank Dr. N. Annandale, the specimens of *Glessula* included under No. 80 of Nevill's ·Hand-list,· i. p. 170. They comprise ten glass-tubes, numbered :—

3631 and 3633, from Chittagong, both labelled " *naja*," a name
    I retain.

3632, from Cachar.

3636. Dikrang, 2000 ft., Dafla Hills: true *subhebes*, G.-A.

3634, no locality : "*macera*" Blf., Assam; name retained and
    described. (Type.)

3338, Naga, Assam: is *mastersi*, G.-A.

3637, no locality: *mastersi* G.-A.

3339, Assam, W. Blf. "*macera*": is *mastersi*, G.-A.

3635, no locality : *naja*. G.-A.

3640, Naga Hills : is *mastersi*, G.-A.

When Nevill wrote he considered them all the same and a new
species ; but it must be remembered that when Nevill was working
at this genus the same critical examination was not made of the
shells, such as Pilsbry advised and adopted. The apex and sculpture was never looked at except with a hand-lens ; a microscope
was never in use. I was employed for six months in 1876–1877
in the Indian Museum, and saw Nevill constantly at work and
occasionally worked with him.

This has caused much confusion, for he also appears to have dis-
tributed them under the name of " *naja*." Under this title he sent
a specimen to Mr. Pilsbry, who describes and figures it in ' Manual
of Conchology,' 2nd Series, Pulmonata, p. 90, pl. 12. f. 10, as
"*naja*" from " Assam." This turns out to be the Chittagong
species. Pilsbry's shell is undoubtedly from Assam ; his description as well as the figure is so good, it verifies the locality. He
says, as to the sculpture :—" Glimpses of excessively weak close
spiral granule-lines may be seen in places." I had not noted this
myself, but I now see the character in my type-specimen of a
Dafla Hill *Glessula subhebes*, an MS. name of G. Nevill's which I
had adopted.

On the other hand, the receipt of these shells in exactly the
state Nevill left them (and he did a great deal of work on the
genus, before he had to retire from the Service, especially on
species from Southern India sent to him by Colonel Beddome) has
cleared up the history and brought to light another species. In
August 1880, Nevill, writing to me, said, No. 80 of his ' Hand-list '
was *G. macera*, and I took this to be his MS. name for the lot
until he should describe it. I have not come across the name in
the Blanford collection nor in Blanford's original catalogue. It is
interesting to record that Nos. 3631 and 3339 both bear this name
on the labels in the glass tubes, and on that in 3634 Nevill has
written "*A. macera*, Blf.," so we know the author. It turns out
that the two tubes contain different species, and 3634 is a mixed
lot of two species ; for the very elongate, flat-sided form of one of
these the name *macera* is most applicable, while it is not so for the
more tumid shape of the other, which is *mastersi*. This fixes the
habitat as Assam, and on looking through the Blanford collection I
find two unnamed *Glessulæ* (No. 842.06.1.1 B.M.), the habitat
Assam, agreeing well in size and form with " *macera*."

GLESSULA NEVILLIANA, n. sp. (Plate CLXI. figs. 11, 12, 13; Plate CLXIV. fig. 3, apex.) No. 449. Type.

Locality. Toruputu Peak, Dafla Hills (4 specimens) (*Godwin-Austen*).

Shell elongately conical; sculpture, coarse somewhat irregular striation; colour: two ruddy, two dull ochraceous; spire high, apex blunt; suture impressed; whorls 9, sides flatly convex; aperture narrowly ovate; peristome thin; columella rather straight, curved, short.

Size: Type .... maj. diam. 5·0   length 17·0 mm.   whorls 9.

Nevill gives for specimens in Indian Museum :—

	maj. diam.	length	whorls
	4·0	13·0 mm.	8.
Small ruddy sp. (fig. 13)	4·0	12·0	
Large sp. with apex broken	5·0	14·0	

7 whorls left (fig. 12).

In this last, from last suture to base of aperture 7 mm., as against 5½ in the Type.

This species is recorded by Nevill in his revised copy of the ' Hand-list,' opposite page 170, as "*Stenogyra (Glessula) austeniana*, Nevill—whorls 8, length 13, diam. 0 mm., one Toruputu, Dafla Hills (Type), coll. Godwin-Austen." The specimen thus named is probably in the Indian Museum. I cannot find that it was ever published: therefore it is now named after my old friend. His early death was a great loss, for he possessed a great knowledge of Indian Mollusca, and had made a close study of the genus *Glessula.*

GLESSULA DIKRANGENSE, n. sp. No. 448 B.M. (Plate CLX. fig. 7.)

Locality. Toruputu Peak, Dafla Hills—in primeval forest. Type. (*Godwin-Austen.*)

Shell elongately turreted; sculpture very fine and close regular striation; colour ochraceous with a strong green tinge; spire long, sides very flatly convex, apex blunt; suture impressed; whorls 9, convexity of side very slight; aperture oval, vertical; peristome strong; columellar margin curving.

Size: maj. diam. 7·75; length 19·0 mm.

In a paper on "The Helicidae of the Dafla Hills" (Jour. Asiat. Soc. Bengal, vol. xlv. pt. ii. 1876, p. 315) I included *Glessula illustris*, the type of which was found on Hengdan Peak in the Naga Hills. This was a hasty determination; after a far more critical one, and a comparison of the photographs of both, it shows considerable difference, sufficient to constitute a new species. The proportion of the last whorl to the length of the axis is very different to that of typical *G. illustris*—taking the axis as 100, it is 100:52.

GLESSULA DIKRANGENSE, n. sp.   No. 3404 B.M.   (Plate CLX. fig. 7 *a*.)

Locality. Toruputu Peak, Dafla Hills (*Godwin-Austen*).

Shell oblongly turreted; sculpture rather strong striation, close and regular; colour dull umber-brown; spire high, apex blunt, side straight; suture impressed; whorls 8, side nearly flat, spire to last whorl 100 : 52·2; aperture oval; columellar margin slightly convex.

Size: maj. diam. 7·0 ; length 17·25 mm.

" DIKRANGIA," genus nov.

Shell very elongate, small, transparent, delicate, turreted with many whorls closely wound and nearly equal in diameter, aperture very small, ovate; animal not known.

GLESSULA (" DIKRANGIA ") NEVILLI, G.-A.

When describing the Helicidæ of the Dafla Hills (J. A. S. B. 1876, vol. xlv. pt. 2, pl. viii. f. 12, p. 315) I put this species into the genus *Opeas*. This determination has been followed by Mr. G. K. Gude in the 'Fauna British India, Mollusca,' vol. ii. 1914, p. 360. Closer attention shows the aperture to be decidedly that of a *Glessula*, but the general form departs much from that genus—so much so, it might well be placed in a distinct subsection. This would be better left to be done when the anatomy of the animal is known to us. I think it better to consider it a new subgenus, and name it " *Dikrangia*," coming after *G. baculina* and *G. garoense*.

The original description, which is as follows, was short and requires amendment—it was not drawn up on one-type shells, but on a set—often done in those early days.

Original description:— "Shell turreted, very elongate, pale, silky with a *green tinge*, older specimens of a pale straw-colour, covered with a thin epidermis, *beautifully striate under lens*. Whorls 11–12, moderately rounded and very gradually diminishing in size to the apex, which is bluish; suture impressed; aperture angular above, outer lip thin.

" Alt. 0·55"; major diam. 0·10".   Largest specimens 0·90".

" *Habitat.* This very delicate elongate shell was common on Toruputu Peak, but far finer specimens, equal in size to the figure, were obtained on the banks of the Pichola Nulla out in the plains. I am not satisfied with this figure, the whorls being rather too flat and the apex too sharp.

" I have named this shell after my friend Mr. G. Nevill, with whom I have now so long been associated in the study and collection of Indian land-shells."

Amended description.

GLESSULA NEVILLI, G.-A.   No. 447 B.M.

Locality. Toruputu Peak, Dafla Hills (*Godwin-Austen*).
Shell finely elongate, turreted; sculpture, well-marked close irregular striation; colour white; spire very slender and lengthened, apex blunt; suture impressed; whorls 12, the six last almost equal in diameter; aperture small, narrowly and vertically ovate; columellar margin convex.
Size: maj. diam. 2·25; length 14 mm.
Var. *major*, G.-A., Pichola Nulla, Durrang District. This has a very smooth surface with very indistinct striation, and has a green tinge. The largest specimen measures 17·75 mm. in length by 3·5, and has 12 whorls.

Although I refer to the Toruputu habitat of the Granite Peak on the main mountain mass 7322 feet above sea-level, and the Pichola Nulla low down and quite out in the plains, I now note, 40 years later, there is a difference something more than "far finer specimens," and that those from the Granite Peak are very different, particularly in size, proportion, and sculpture. Many conchologists would consider them distinct species however, it is sufficient that *G. nevilli* stands for the mountain form, the one first found by me, and that of the plains be considered a variety *major*.

3 a. The Miri Hills.

From the great Valley of the Subansiri no species of *Glessula* have been received; it is a large unworked area of 2500 sq. miles.

4. Eastern Assam with the Singpho Hills and Patkoi Range.

Glessula maiamensis, n. sp.   Pl. CLX. figs. 10–11.
              dihingensis, n. sp.   Pl. CLXIV. fig. 4 (apex).

GLESSULA MAIAMENSIS, n. sp.   No. 1737.   (Plate CLX. fig. 10.) Type.

Locality. Maiam Peak, Singpho Hills; a single specimen (*M. Ogle*).
Shell oblongly turreted, rather tumid; sculpture: strong, rather distant, engraved striation, showing strong near suture; colour ochraceous with a greenish tint; spire elongately conoid,

apex very blunt and rounded, sides flatly convex; suture moderately impressed; whorls 7. sides very flatly convex; aperture oval; peristome outer tip thickened; columellar margin slightly convex, nearly straight.

Size: maj. diam. 9·5; length 22 mm.

The above peak, a trigonometrical station, is situated on the watershed of the Patkai Range and is 6900 feet in altitude. It was first visited in the cold season of 1884-85 by Colonel Woodthorpe, R.E., with his assistant Mr. Ogle, and they were accompanied by Mr. Tom D. La Touche of the Geological Survey, who published an excellent account of Geology of the Upper Dihing Basin, Singpho Hills.

GLESSULA MAIAMENSIS, n. sp.   (Plate CLX. fig. 11.)   No. 29 B.M.

Locality. Diyung Valley, Singpho Hills: two specimens (*M. T. Ogle*).

Shell is more elongate than the type; colour is greener; side of spire rather flatter; aperture rounder, from the outer lip having more convexity.   All the kind of diversity the shells of this genus present, particularly when a large series is obtainable.

Size: maj. diam. 8·5; alt. axis 20·8 mm.

GLESSULA DIHINGENSIS, n. sp.

Locality. Dihing Valley, Assam (type No. 3251 B.M.); some ten specimens (*M. T. Ogle*). No. 1600 B.M. from Sonari Tea Garden, near Sadiya. (Plate CLXIV. fig. 4, apex.)

Shell elongate, turreted: sculpture: very smooth generally, fine, close, rather strong ribbing near and below the suture; colour umber-brown; spire long and fine; suture impressed: whorls 10, the last short; aperture ovate, small; columellar margin well curved.

Size: maj. diam. 5·0; length 18·0 mm.

This is not unlike *G. macera*, but the whorls are not so close and the last is longer in proportion to those above, *i.e.*, a more tumid basal one.   Specimens from Sadiya (No. 3151 B.M., 10 in number, collected by my old assistant Mr. Ogle) differ in colour, being a very pale ash, the largest of 9 whorls measures 21 × 5·25 mm.   I have also two examples from Sonari Tea Garden, 15·5 mm. in length, sent me by Mr. S. E. Peale, very finely and closely striated.

4 a. *Abor Hills and Tsanspu Valley.*

GLESSULA OAKESI, G.-A.

Records of the Indian Museum, vol. viii. pt. xii. No. 49, p. 617, figs. 8 A, B, C, D.

Locality. Abor Hills (*Captain G. F. T. Oakes, R.E.*) No. 3600 B.M. Type. (Plate CLX. fig. 15 × 1·56.)

Original Description :—" Shell oblong turreted, shining surface ; sculpture : regular somewhat distant incised lines ; colour ochraceous one umber brown : spire high, sides very flatly convex ; suture impressed ; whorls 7, flatly convex, proportion of body whorl to length 100 : 2·5; aperture rather narrowly oval, peristome outer lip thickened ; columellar margin slightly convex."

" Size : maj. diam. 7·0 ; alt. axis 16·5 mm."

" Two specimens of this species, though rather smaller in size and not fully grown, were sent to me from Brahmakund by Mr. M. Ogle, No. 3578 B.M. coll. The largest measures 11 × 5 mm. The species was received alive in 1913, from Captain Oakes with other species and dissected." No doubt the first *Glessula* so received in this country ; a few lived for some months until the winter set in, feeding on lettuce, etc.

" Animal of *Glessula oakesi* from Rotung (Oakes). The sole of the foot is crossed by coarse ridges, there is a very distinct peripodial margian (text-fig. 3 A). The genitalia (figs. 8 B, C, D) was fairly well seen in one specimen, but more material was sadly wanted. The hermaphrodite duct is conspicuous from its size and close convolution, bound closely together at its junction with the albumen gland. The penis is very short with a short stout flagellum terminating in three blunt knots ; it thus differs from what I have been able to see in other species. The vas deferens is given off from near the head of the penis, the spermatheca was not seen."

" This species (*G. oakesi*) is the same as the one recorded from Rotung as *G. botellus*, Bs., of Southern India by Mr. H. B. Preston in the ' Records of the Indian Museum,' vol. viii., Nov. 1915, p. 539; it is a bare record, in any case remarkable as regards range. As I had not noticed this South Indian species among the large series sent me from the Abor Hills, I was anxious to see the shells which had gone to Calcutta. Dr. Annandale very kindly sent these to me (October, 1916), and I have compared them with specimens of *Glessula botellus* in the Henry Blanford collection from the Nilgiris, with the result that I cannot confirm Mr. Preston's determination. This Abor *Glessula* (*oakesi*) is decidedly smaller than *G. botellus*, and not so tumid, the whorls are closer wound, the outer lip is much more thickened than in *botellus*, the larger shell. I have compared the embryonic whorls and made enlarged drawings of *botellus*, Nilgiris (Pl. CXLIII. fig. 1), of Mr. Preston's specimen (Pl. CXLIII. fig. 3), and of the type specimen of *oakesi* (Pl. CXLIII. fig. 2) ; the difference between the first and the two last is very marked, it is unmistakable."

An example rather more tumid was received from Capt. Oakes (No. 3158 B.M.), and one came from near the Serpo River bridge (No. 3053 B.M.).

GLESSULA ABORENSIS, G.-A. 3103 B.M. Type. (Plate CXLII. fig. 4.)

Rec. Indian Museum, 1918, vol. viii. pt. xii. No. 49, p. 618.

Locality. Abor Hills; five specimens (*Capt. G. F. T. Oakes, R.E.*).

Original description:—"Shell elongately turreted, sides nearly straight : sculpture : very regular striation, less apparent on the last whorl : colour dark chestnut-brown in the type-shell, more ochraceous in others; spire attenuate, apex blunt : suture impressed; whorls 8, sides flatly convex ; aperture ovate; peristome outer lip thin, with strong convexity ; columellar margin nearly straight, feeble, slightly truncated.

" Size : maj. diam. 5·0 ; alt. axis 16·25 mm.

" This species varies in form, some being less attenuate, but all have the blunt apex and similar sculpture."

---

5. *Garo, Kasi, and Jaintia Hills.*

Glessula tenuispira, Bs.	Pl. CLIX. fig. 3.
subauculina, n. sp.	Pl. CLIX. figs. 4, 9.
=*theobaldi,* Hanley MS.	
garoense, n. sp.	Pl. CLIX. fig. 15.
small var.	Pl. CLXX. fig. 11.
manipurense, var.	
subhastula, n. sp.	Pl. CLXI. fig. 18. / Pl. CLXIII. fig. 15.
crassilabris, Bs.	Pl. CLX. figs. 14, 17, 18, 19, 20. / Pl. CLXIV. figs. 16, 17. / Pl. CLX. fig. 17.
var. *nana.*	Pl. CLXII. fig. 23.
pyramis, Bs.	Pl. CLX. fig. 24.
hanleyi, n. sp.	Pl. CLXII. fig. 16.
solidus, n. sp.	Pl. CLXII. fig. 8.
Judukamia abnormis, n. sp.	Pl. CLX. figs. 22, 23.

GLESSULA TENUISPIRA, Benson.

Colonel Beddome, in his Monograph of the Genus (Pro. Malacol. Soc. vol. vii. 1906, p. 160), records this species from many localities all very distant from each other, viz., Darjiling, Pegu, N. Canara, Khasi, and Dafla Hills. In a paper by Benson in the 'Annals and Magazine of Natural History' (1860), he gives a list of all the Continental-Indian species of *Achatina*—in which *A. tenuispira* appears as from the Khasia Hills, Darjiling, and Burma ; he says also " In Burmah Mr. Theobald got a variety of *A. tenuispira* on the banks of the Irawady." I have for long doubted that this species has such an extended range. Beddome even goes further and considers *G. baculina*, Hy. Blanford "only a more slender form of *tenuispira*" (Pl. CLIX. figs. 1, 2); he could not possibly have seen the types of the former species—the shell from the Khasi Hills (Teria Ghat) (Pl. CLIX. fig. 3) differs altogether from the Sikhim one, and when they are placed side by side the points of difference are seen at once. I still more doubt the extension of *tenuispira* to North Canara as well as to Pegu. In J. A. S. B. 1865, p. 95, Blanford says *Achatina tenuispira*, Bens., of small size is common at Akouktoung and farther south. I refer to this under *Glessula pertenuis*, No. 8, East of Bay of Bengal. I have not at present the shells to examine. Geoffrey Nevill, 'Hand List,' i. 1878, p. 169, records Darjiling, also Khasi and Dafla Hills; from these two last localities the shells were of my collecting, for when Nevill was studying the genus I supplied him liberally with specimens.

The first record of *G. tenuispira* appears in a paper entitled "Descriptive Catalogue of Terrestrial and Fluviatile Testacea, chiefly from the North-East Frontier of Bengal," by W. H. Benson, Journal of Asiatic Society Bengal. June 1836, p. 350.

(The Collection was purchased by the Asiatic Society in 1833.)

No. 11. in the List.—*Achatina tenuispira.*

Original description :—" *Testa elongata turrita, cornea, longitudinaliter striata, rersus apicem attenuata, columnari, anfracta ultimo interdum facilis, quibusdam albidis transversis ornato, suturis impressis apice obtuso.*

" Long. 1 poll. circiter ; Lat. 0·55.

" This Achatina, belonging to De Ferussac's subgenus *Cochlicopa* and to his group of *Hyloides*, is remarkable for the attenuated columellar form of the terminal whorls of the spire."

(Followed by No. 12, *Crassilabris*).

At the time this description was written, Benson had not seen a Darjiling specimen; he was then Magistrate and Collector of Sylhet, and there can be no doubt whatever typical *tenuispira* came from that district—most probably from that rich collecting place Teria Ghat, which lies on its northern boundary, where Benson also obtained the very well-marked species *G. crassilabris.*

We are apt to forget how much we owe to Benson and Hutton, the pioneers in Indian Malacology, who, with little assistance and encouragement, did so much. Looking back to the early thirties and the many papers Benson lived to publish, it is noticeable how much his remarks increase the interest in the species he discovered, how much is suggested as to relationship and distribution. The brothers Blanford followed with the same scientific treatment. In comparison the record of to-day, with few exceptions, is bald to a degree, owing to a want of knowledge of the physical features of the country, its size, and varying climatic conditions.

GLESSULA TENUISPIRA, Bs. Coll. Hy. Blf., No. 11.9.iii.15 B.M. (Plate CLIX. fig. 3.)

Locality. Teria Ghat, Khasi.

Henry Blanford's collection contains 4 specimens from that place, and I have 10 others (No. 1616 B.M.) collected by myself. The largest of these measures 31 mm. long by 8½ breadth at the aperture. It differs in form very considerably from what has been hitherto known as *tenuispira* of Darjiling and Sikhim, which I have named and separated as *longispira.*

GLESSULA (RISHETIA) TENUISPIRA, Bs. 11.9.iii.15 B.M. (Plate CLIX. fig. 3.)

Locality. Teria Ghat, foot of Khasi Hills (*ex coll. H. F. Blanford*).

Shell elongately turreted; sculpture striation distant, closer, finer, and regular towards the apex; colour ochraceous, with decided green tint; spire long, apex rather blunt, sides nearly straight, slight convexity; suture impressed; whorls 10·5, slightly convex, proportion of spire to last whorl 100: 29; aperture oval; columellar margin rather straight.

Size: major diam. 9·0; length 29·0 mm.

I obtained this species at Teria Ghat and also in the West Khasi Hills, some dozen specimens (No. 1582 B.M.), the largest being 33 mm. in length.

GLESSULA (RISHETIA) TENUISPIRA, Bs., var. No. 3332 B.M.

Locality. Garo Hills, a single specimen (*Godwin-Austen*).

Shell more slender in form; sculpture smoother than the Teria Ghat examples of *tenuispira*; colour ochraceous umber-brown; spire, apex fine; whorls 11, 100: 40·4; aperture narrowly ovate.

Size: maj. diam. 8·0; length 27·25 mm.

Specimen from above Tura, 10 × 29·8.

It is of considerable interest to note that Mr. S. W. Kemp, of the Indian Museum, has recently collected *Glessula tenuispira* at Tura in the Garo Hills, extending its range from Teria Ghat thus far to the west some 100 miles. Throughout this distance, the conditions are the same (tropical forest and for half the year excessive rainfall) on the steep spurs overlooking the great marshes of Sylhet and Mymensing. Dissection shows the animal to have all the characters of the species I describe under *longispira* of Darjiling and Sikhim. It marks the western extension of the subgenus—this also falls in with the geological evidence we possess, that the Garo–Khasi area was in early Tertiary time much more intimately connected with the South-Eastern Himalaya on the north and not so markedly cut off as now by the broad low valley of the Brahmaputra, filled with alluvial deposits of great thickness.

GLESSULA (RISHETIA) SUBACULINA, n. sp., Coll. G.-A. No. 3555
B.M. (Plate CLIX. fig. 9.)

Locality. Landomodo Trigonometrical Station. Type. N. Khasi
Hills (7 specimens); The Maotherichan Ridge (No. 3556) (4 specimens): South Jaintia (1 specimen). Tura, Garo Hills (*S. W. Kemp*).

Shell elongately turreted; sculpture irregular, well-developed
rather coarse striation, but varying much in different shells;
colour ochraceous; spire elongate, sides flatly convex, apex blunt;
suture rather shallow; whorls 12, sides not quite flat; aperture
narrowly ovate; columella curving subobliquely, broadly truncate.
Size: maj. diam. 7·25: length 31·0 mm.

This approaches the Sikhim *G. baculina* Bs., but is rather
broader than that species, the whorls near apex increasing more
rapidly. It is not so smooth and shiny.

No. 77 of Nevill's ' Hand-list,' p. 170, *Gless. baculina*—3 Khasi
Hills, presented by me, are *subaculina*; they have been sent home
(1916) by Dr. N. Annandale and compared by me.

GLESSULA (RISHETIA) SUBACULINA, G.-A., No. 1580 B.M. (Plate
CLIX. fig. 4.)

Conch. Ind. pl. xvii. fig 5 as *G. theobaldi*, Hanley MSS.

Locality. Teria Ghat, foot of Khasi Hills (*Godwin-Austen*).

Shell elongately turreted, slender; sculpture: striation of growth
strongest below the suture and most regular on the 5th and 6th
whorls; colour umber-brown or dull ochraceous; spire elongate,
apex fine; suture shallow; whorls 12, sides flat, proportion spire
to last whorl 100: 24·4; aperture narrowly ovate; peristome
outer lip thin; columellar margin regularly convex, not solid.
Size: maj. diam. 9·5; alt. axis 34·75 mm.

There are two specimens in my collection now in the Natural
History Museum (No. 1580 B.M.); their history is of interest and
important with regard to the exact habitat of *G. theobaldi*,
Hanley.

Considerable confusion surrounds this species, owing to the
authors of the 'Conchologia Indica' working apart when it was
passing through the press—one (Mr. Hanley) in England, the other
(Mr. Theobald) in India, dealing with shells from two very different
localities. Hanley first describes the shell very briefly of *Achatina
theobaldi*, Conch. Ind. p. 9, 1870; in explanation of pl. xvii. fig. 5,
from "Near the Salwen," he says, "Differs from *A. cassiaca*, of which
it has been considered a variety, by its smoothness, more convex
whorls, &c." The shell was therefore a *Bacillum*, and we can
presume the species recorded by Theobald from the Shan States was
also a *Bacillum, vide* a paper in the ' Journal of the Asiatic Society
of Bengal,' 1870 (not 1871 as given by Gude), vol. xxxix. p. 395.
On land-shells from the Shan States and Pegu as *Achatina (Glessula)*

theobaldiana, Hanley, the footnote Conch. Indica, pl. xvii. fig. 5, shows us that that work was published and had been seen by him. In 'Nevill's Hand-list,' p. 172, we find " No. 102 *Stenogyra* (*Glessula*) *theobaldi*, Hanley, 2, Salween, coll. Mr. Theobald." Nevill puts them in *Bacillum*. It is to be hoped these specimens are still in the Indian Museum, for they are very valuable; they would clear up where true *Glessula theobaldi* comes from. Hanley figured it on pl. xvii, but in the index to *Achatina* in the Conch. Indica, p. xii, to *theobaldi* there is a footnote "2" "from Teria Ghat." It looks as if Hanley had substituted another species for figuring, and not taken the Shan one, under the impression they were one and the same. I am glad I am able to clear this up to a certain extent, and show how a Khasi Hill form has got introduced. When Hanley was engaged on the 'Conchologia Indica' I sent him a number of species of *Glessula* both named and unnamed, which he afterwards returned to me. Among them I have two specimens of a *Glessula* named *Theobaldi*—in Handley's handwriting—from Teria Ghat (No. 1580, Godwin-Austen Collection, British Museum). At the time I lent Hanley my *Glessula* I had not a single species of the genus in my collection from the Salween Valley, so there could be no mingling of specimens. Turning to pl. xvii., it may be noted at once that the shells are all enlarged; take, for example, *G. orobia* (fig. 7) and *G. prælustris* (fig. 6). *G. theobaldi* (fig. 5) has a very considerable likeness to the Teria Ghat shell which Hanley returned to me with that name, allowing for similar enlargement with the sculpture also somewhat exaggerated. At the same time fig. 5 has not at all the form of a *Bacillum*, measuring 42 mm. as given by Mr. Gude (ex icon); on the contrary, it has a fine attenuate apex and not the characteristic blunt rounded one of *Bacillum* (*vide* drawing by same artist, Mr. G. B. Sowerby, of *B. cassiaca* with its flat sides). All this points to fig. 5 representing the Teria Ghat specimen, and it is quite possible the one photographed for me by Mr. T. S. Gladstone (Pl. CLIX. fig. 4) is the identical shell.

Theobald's shells from the Salween, in the Indian Museum, cleared this up; for on making application for them to Dr. N. Annandale, the present Superintendent, he has most obligingly sent them to me (March 1916); the label is in type, a cutting from p. 172. They belong, as Nevill records them, to the genus *Bacillum*; they are both immature, the largest of 9 whorls, measuring 23·25 mm. in length, with sides of greater convexity than in *B. cassiaca*, distinguishing it at once. The typical specimen sent home by Theobald to Hanley would appear to have been lost; it is fortunate that about the same time Theobald gave specimens to the Indian Museum.

I found in the Beddome Collection (No. 121) a single, also immature shell, with a label " sent by Theobald as '*Salwiniana*.'" On comparison with the specimens of *B. theobaldi*, Hanley, from Calcutta, I consider it the same; it is only 21 mm. in length. Mr. Gude had marked it " young of *cassiaca* Bs."

GLESSULA (RISHETIA) GAROENSE, n. sp. (Plate CLIX. fig. 15.)

Locality: South Garo Hills. Type. No. 1595 B.M. (*Godwin-Austen*).

Shell attenuately turreted, sides flat, thin; sculpture, surface very smooth, a few distant transverse shallow engraved lines, differing from the usual raised striæ; colour pale umber-brown; spire fine; apex very attenuate, first 4 whorls with same diameter (Pl. CLXIV. fig. 5); suture shallow; whorls 13, sides flatly convex, there is but little difference in the diameter at the 9th whorl and the last; aperture narrowly ovate; peristome thin, a callous on the body whorl; columellar margin oblique, very slight in structure.

Size: maj. diam. 5·0; total length 27·25 mm.

In form it is similar to *G. baculina*, var. *exilis* of Sikhim; the apex is not so attenuate, the whorls are flatter, and the sculpture differs considerably. In the Sikhim form there is much raised striation.

Under No. 68, p. 169, of 'Nevill's Hand-list,' 2 specimens from the Garo Hills are recorded under *G. pertennis*; they were presented unnamed by me. These have been kindly sent home for comparison by Dr. N. Annandale, to whom my best thanks are due; they are this species *garoense*. On this data in the 'Hand-list,' Mr. Gude in 'Fauna British India' extends the range of *G. pertennis*, a Pegu species, to the Assam Range; such record of distribution is valueless.

GLESSULA (RISHETIA) GAROENSE, G.-A.

Locality. South Jaintia; 4 specimens, No. 3562 (*Godwin-Austen*).

Shell attenuately turreted; sculpture, striation very fine and close, disappearing in full-grown shells; colour dull umber-brown; spire tapering evenly; whorls 12.

Size: maj. diam. 5·5; length 26·75 mm.

At first sight there is a remarkable similarity between this species and *G. pertennis*, Wm. Blanford, of Bassein, but it disappears under the microscope. The apical whorls are not alike, and the aperture differs still more on the columellar margin and truncation.

GLESSULA (RISHETIA) GAROENSE, G.-A., small var. (Plate CLIX. fig. 11.)

Locality. Naraindhur, Cachar; 11 specimens. Type. No. 1657 (*F. Ede*).

This measures 20·5 mm. in length and 4·5 mm. in maj. diam. It is of a darker umber than typical *garoense*, and has the very smooth surface of that shell: 12 whorls, sides slightly more convex; apex very fine, first 4 whorls hardly increase at all (Pl. CLXIV. fig. 6).

I am fortunate in having specimens in spirit of a small elongate many-whorled species from Silchar, Cachar, sent me by Mr. F. Ede.

(The sole of the foot very closely segmented.) I have been successful in getting out the genitalia, but in a detached state. The specimen contained 8 well-formed eggs in the oviduct; they measure 1·5 mm. in diameter, perfect globes. The penis (Plate CLXV. fig. 6) has an elongate simple sheath, with a very small flagellum, close to the vas deferens attachment at the distal end. The spermatheca (fig. 6 *a*) was elongate with a bulbous end; the penis is thus similar to that of *G. longispira* of Sikhim, and it may ultimately be found that all the elongate turreted *Glessula* will have this type of male organ distinguishing them from that of *G. ochracea*, &c. The formula of the radula is:

$$20 . 7 . 1 . 7 . 20 \text{ or } 27 . 1 . 27.$$

The centre tooth has a long narrow plate with a small cusp at the base; the admedian are of the same shape as in *G. longispira*; the marginals are very numerous, becoming very minute on the outer edge. There are no intermediate teeth; the admedian merge into the marginals.

GLESSULA SUBHASTULA, n. sp. (Plate CLXI. fig. 18; Plate CLXIII. fig. 15, apex.)

Locality. Nongsingriang, North Khasi Hills; No. 3551 B.M. Type (*Godwin-Austen*).

Shell elongately;conoid: sculpture irregular, fine close, very well-defined transverse striation (not so regular as in *G. hastula*); colour dark ochraceous; spire long attenuate (less so than *hastula*), apex fine (larger than in *hastula*); suture impressed: whorls 7½, sides flatly convex; aperture very narrow, vertical; peristome thin; columellar margin nearly straight.

Size: Type. Maj. diam. 3·25; length 9·0 mm. apex.
N. Khasi sp. (3546' B.M.) „ 3·5 „ 10·75 „
largest (3557 B.M.) „ 3·50 „ 12·0 „

I first found this species (No. 3549 B.M., enlarged apex, Pl. CLXIII. fig. 14), which I then took to be *hastula* of Benson, in the deep valley to the east of Cherra Poonjee the first summer I passed there. Two specimens were returned to me by Mr. Sylvanus Hanley, in whose hands I placed a number of species of *Glessula* when he was working on the ' Conchologia Indica '—this No. 3546' (Pl. CLXI. fig. 19) was returned to me with a note in pencil "allied to *subfusiformis*, W. Blf." A single specimen of *subhastula* was also found in the Dunsiri Valley below Samaguting.

I have received a specimen from Mr. S. W. Kemp found at Tura, Garo Hills.

GLESSULA SUBHASTULA, G.-A., var. type (Plate CLXI. fig. 19.)

Locality. North Khasi: No. 3546 (*Godwin-Austen*).

Shell elongately conoid; sculpture regular, quite strong striation; colour rich umber-brown: spire long, sides flattened, apex blunt rounded; suture impressed; whorls 7½, sides flattened; aperture rather narrow: peristome slightly thickened; columellar margin nearly vertical, not truncated.

Size: maj. diam. 3·6; alt. axis 10·4 mm.

This is much stouter and with a much blunter apex than typical *subhastula*, with the aperture not so narrow; 9 specimens were found on Hinriutinoh Peak, North Cachar Hills.

No. 2026 B.M., apex enlarged (Pl. CLXIII. fig. 12).

No. 3557, North Khasi, apex enlarged (Pl. CLXIII. fig. 11).

GLESSULA ILLUSTRIS, G.-A. 3076 B.M. type.

Journ. Asiat. Soc. Bengal, vol. xliv. 2. 1875, p. 3. (Plate i. fig. 5.) Figured in 'Conchologia Indica,' 1875, pl. cii. fig. 9. Nevill, 'Hand-list,' i. 1878, p. 170, 7 sp., Hengdan.

Original description:—"Shell elongately oval, greenish horny, finely striated longitudinally; whorls 7, very slightly rounded; suture moderately impressed; the lip thickened; columellar margin slightly curved and strong; apex blunt."

" Length 0·75; maj. diam. 0·3; length of aperture 0·3 in.

Hab. Hengdan Peak, North Cachar Hills, at 6843 feet, in forest, also near Nenglo, at 6000 feet, and in the Lukah Valley, Jaintia Hills, at 1000 feet.

" This species is an elongate and larger form of *Glessula crassilabris*, Bs., of which *G. pyramis* is a closer variety; but its much more elongate form and stronger striation make it a good connecting species with *G. butleri*, described further on. The form from the Lukah Valley is a tumid departure from the type figured (var. *tumida*, G.-A.).

" One specimen—alt. 0·75; maj. diam. 0·38 in.

Another ,, ,, 0·65 ,, 0·35 ,.

" I look on all these species as proper varieties, and *G. crassilabris*, very abundant in all the grass country of the Khasi Hills, may be taken as the type; a difference in elevation and condition of habitat, from damp dark forest to hot grassy slopes, having produced modifications of form."

Amended description.

GLESSULA ILLUSTRIS, G.-A. Type. No. 3076 B.M. (Plate CLX. fig. 12.)

Locality. Hengdan Peak, North Cachar Hills (*Godwin-Austen*).

Shell elongately oval, rather solid, smooth; sculpture: distant, fine irregular striae, fine on the apical whorls; colour deep olivaceous, with an ochre tint; spire high, sides flatly convex, apex blunt; suture moderately impressed; whorls 7, very flatly convex, rather tumid; aperture rather narrowly oval, vertical; peristome thickened, but not so strongly as in *G. crassilabris*; columellar margin straightly curved. Size: maj. diam. 8·0; length 19·2 mm.

The last whorl up to the suture is ample; it measures from the base of the columella in front to the suture 11·50 mm., proportion in terms of 100 is 100 : 60. The range on which it was found was covered for miles with magnificent forest.

GLESSULA ILLUSTRIS, G.-A.

I have looked at the type after reading Pilsbry's remarks on this species (Man. Conch. ser. 2, xx. 1909, p. 95, pl. ii. figs. 13–16). The vertical striation and grooving is irregular, but this is generally the case in the genus; on the apical whorls it is more regular. There is certainly fine spiral striation, but it is indistinct and not to be seen in some specimens; the suture is also not always crenulate. The striation on the embryonic whorls is very similar to that in *crassilabris*. The examples from the Luka Valley in the Jaintia Hills (3078 B.M.) may be very well considered a var. *tumida*.

Beddome erroneously considered it the same as *G. facula* of Southern India.

GLESSULA ILLUSTRIS, var. TUMIDA, G.-A.   (Plate CLX. fig. 13.)

Locality. Lukah Valley, Jaintia Hills.   No. 3078 B.M. (*Godwin-Austen*).

Shell ovate; sculpture: regular, incised striation, somewhat distant; colour strong ochraceous with slight olivaceous tint; spire moderately high, conic, sides flatly convex; suture rather shallow; whorls 7½, the last tumid, sides slightly convex; aperture widely oval, vertical; peristome slightly thickened; columellar margin rather short, subvertical.

Size: maj. diam. 13·75; length 16·2 mm.; length to body whorl 100 : 62.

GLESSULA CRASSILABRIS, Bs.   3435 B.M.   (Plate CLX. fig. 17.)

Locality. Teria Ghat (*Godwin-Austen*).

Shell conically turreted, glassy; sculpture: distant, strong, transverse striæ, very irregular as regards distribution and relief, near suture, very fine; colour bright ochraceous with a green tint; spire fine and pointed, sides flatly convex; suture well impressed; whorls 7½, with considerable convexity; aperture ovate; peristome outer margin well thickened; columellar margin concave.

Size: (Sp. figured) maj. diam. 6·0; alt. axis 13·4 mm.
The largest   „   „   7·2;   „   14·75 „

Note from Field Book.—Animal with tentacles black throughout, body short, under side of foot pale yellow. The largest specimens were obtained in North Khasi, near Simleng on the Lubah River, in the high grass of old jooms, *i.e.* the clearings of virgin forest, first cut down, then burnt and cultivated.

This species has locally an extended range, compared with other species, and it varies much in size, form, and colour. It is a very common species at Teria Ghat, the original locality, and I found it in the following places, specimens from which are figured.

No. 3552.   From North Khasi.
One very large specimen figured 16 × 8·25 mm.   (Plate CLX. fig. 14.)

3435 B.M.   Teria Ghat.   Typical locality.   (Plate CLXIV. fig. 16, apex.)

Specimen figured 13 × 6·25 mm., apex very fine, ochraceous. (Plate CLX. fig. 17.)

452 B.M.   Shengorh Peak, Dafla Hills.

crassilabris, var.: the sculpture differs from that of typical shells in being much closer.

Specimen figured 13·50 × 6·25 mm.; four obtained, all of a pale chrysophase green tint. (Plate CLX. fig. 19.)

3553 B.M.   Jaintia.

Largest specimen figured 14·5 × 6·20 mm., strong ochraceous, sculpture distant striation. (Plate CLX. fig. 18.)

3390 B.M.   Garo Hills.

Specimen figured 9 × 4·50 mm., very small, ovately turreted, dark umber-brown with a green tinge. (Plate CLX. fig. 20.)

From other localities I have :—

3372 B.M.   Garo Hills.

Largest specimen 14·20 × 7·0 mm., dark ochraceous.

3428 B.M.   North Cachar.

Largest 13·25 × 6·0 mm., ochraceous with slight green tint.

3388 B.M.   Gowhathi, Assam.

10·20 × 5·0 mm., ochraceous with slight greenish tint.

3569 B.M.   Naga Hills, under Laisom Peak.

15·0 × 6·75 mm., apex blunt, more elongate than type, greenish ochre; 7 whorls.

452 B.M.   Dafla Hills, Shengor Peak. (Plate CLXIV. fig. 17, apex.)

Very fine spiral striæ on the apical whorl (not shown in fig.).

453 B.M.   Dafla Hills, in the Burroi Gorge.

10·50 × 4·80 mm., dark umber, with green tinge decidedly olivaceous, more elongate, very distinct spiral striæ on the apical whorl.

913 B.M.   Khasi.

10·25 × 50 mm., 7 whorls, ochraceous, apex rather blunt.

Blanford writes (J. A. S. B. 1865, p. 95): " A small variety of *A. crassilabris*, Bs., occurs in Arakan, and another form perhaps distinct, but closely allied, was found in the Shan Hills near Ava."

Specimens of the first I found unnamed in Henry Blanford's collection collected by Mr. Raban of the Indian Civil Service. I consider them distinct and have named them *G. rabani*. Those from the Shan Hills have come to light in Wm. Blanford's collection (No. 261–06.2.2), five specimens. They are undoubtedly distinct, and I have named the species *G. feddeni* after Mr. Fedden of the Geological Survey of India, who collected largely in that part of Burma.

GLESSULA CRASSILABRIS, Bs., var. NANA.. (Plate CLXII. fig. 23.)
No. 1609 B.M.

Locality. North Khasi (2 specimens) (*Godwin-Austen*).

Shell oblong turreted, smooth and shiny; sculpture: a few incised lines; colour ochraceous with a green tinge; spire elongate, sides convex, apex blunt; suture impressed; whorls 7, slightly convex; aperture narrowly ovate; peristome outer lip thickened slightly; columellar margin short, truncated, rather straight.

Size: maj. diam. 3·8; length 8 mm.

This shell, evidently fully grown, has much the form of *G. crassilabris*, and the sculpture is of similar character, but it is so very much smaller. There being only two specimens it is better to consider them a dwarf variety than to give a specific title. A single specimen was also found in the Jatinga Valley, N. Cachar (No. 3412 B.M.), another on Koliaghur Hill on the L.B. of the Brahmaputra (No. 3567 B.M.), while yet another from the Dunsiri Valley, also at a low elevation (No. 3392 B.M.).

GLESSULA PYRAMIS, Bs. (Plate CLX. fig. 24; Plate CLXIV. fig. 23, apex.)

Locality. Teria Ghat. 3550 G.-A. coll. (*Godwin-Austen*).

Achatina pyramis, Bs.

Original description :—" *Testa oblongo-turrita, solidula, lævigata, striatula, nitida. luteo-corneo: spira turrita, lateribus convexiusculis, apice obtusiusculo, sutura impressa; anfractibus 8, convexiusculis, ultimo $\frac{1}{3}$ testæ æquante, antice obsolete plicato: apertura subverticali, elliptico-semiovali, columella arcuata, callosa, basi oblique truncata, peristomate recto obtuso, intus albido-labiato.*

" Long. 15, diam. 6 mill.; apert. 5 mill. longa, 2¼ lata.

" Habitat ad Teria Ghat Montium Khasi. Detexit W. Theobald.

" Allied to the smaller *Ach. crassula*, B., from Darjiling. but distinguished from it by its colour, smoother sculpture, more convex and numerous whorls, by the characters of the peristome, and by the convex and not planate sides of the spire.

" A large variety of *Ach. crassula*, collected by Mr. W. T. Blanford near Darjiling, is 12 mill. in length by 5¼ in breadth, and, like the type, possesses only seven whorls."

E. pyramis is very smooth and glassy. The largest specimen from Tiria Ghat figured measures 14·5 × 5·75, slightly smaller than the specimen described by Benson.

In the Beddome collection I found a single specimen (No. 747) named *pyramis* by Colonel Beddome: he does not refer to it in his notes on the genus, although its habitat is Ponsec. It measures 17 × 6·8 mm.

This is no doubt the *Glessula pyramis*, var. *major*, of Geoffrey Nevill, 6 sp., Ponsee coll. Dr. J. Anderson, *vide* ' Hand-list,' i. p. 160. In the copy which he gave to me, Nevill has written

" var. *major*, Nevill, 20 × 8 mm. aufr. 9." Besides its much larger size, it differs in many respects from typical *pyramis* in the general shape of the spire, the convexity of the whorls, and the form of the columellar margin, which is more curved and stronger than in *pyramis*, and I therefore name it *G. ponsiensis*. Since writing the above I have received from the Indian Museum the specimens which Nevill dealt with, and have compared them with typical specimens of *G. pyramis* from Teria Ghat, and drawn the apex of both. There is no doubt the Ponsi shell is quite distinct, and has no connection with *pyramis* whatever.

Description of the living animal made in my Field Book of one taken at Teria Ghat is " 0·35″ long, almost colourless, the eye-tentacles only dark coloured, a black line extending from the base of each along the upper side of the neck (this, of course, is the line of the retractor muscle), foot short."

GLESSULA HANLEYI, n. sp. No. 3547 B.M. (Plate CLXII. fig. 16.)

Locality. North Khasi. Type (*Godwin-Austen*).

Shell elongate; sculpture: few and distant extremely fine striæ: colour pale ochraceous; spire high, sides with slight convexity, apex blunt; suture well impressed; whorls 8, side flatly convex; aperture narrow; peristome outer lip thickened; columellar margin vertical, strong, sinuate.

Size : maj. diam. 4·75; length 12 mm.

This shell was seen by Mr. Sylvanus Hanley, after whom I name it; he returned it to me undetermined. It is a single shell, but having a history I am constrained to distinguish it, as I cannot find anything like it. I at first placed it with *G. burakensis*.

GLESSULA SOLIDA, n. sp. No. 3548. B.M. (Plate CLXII. fig. 8.)

Locality. North Khasi Hills and valley east of Cherra Poonjee (*Godwin-Austen*).

Shell oblong conoid, short, solid; sculpture: distant, irregular, fine striation; colour ochraceous; spire elongately conoid, sides convex; suture well impressed; whorls 6, sides convex; aperture ovate, vertical; peristome outer lip very thickened; columellar margin short, convex, well truncated.

Size : maj. diam. 4·0 : length 8·0 mm.

On finding this shell I considered it to be the same as Benson's *orobia*, of Darjiling, but it was not at the time compared with typical specimens. I find now it is very much smaller, very different in its shape and proportions, the side of the spire being much more convex than in the Darjiling shells, with which I have compared it, in the Hy. Blanford collection (No. 17. 9.iii.15 B.M.). (Plate CLXII. fig. 6.)

JADUKAMIA, subgen. nov.

Shell small, short, solid, regularly ribbed, almost costulate; spire elongately conoid; apex bluntly pyramidal, very rounded; columellar margin short, concave, and abruptly truncate.

GLESSULA (JADUKAMIA) ABNORMIS, n. sp. (Plate CLX. fig. 22.) No. 1034, 06. 1–1.

Locality. Khasi Hills (*Godwin-Austen*).

. Shell ovate; sculpture: close, regular, strong ribbing, almost costulate; colour ochraceous, shiny; spire elongately conoid, apex bluntly pyramidal; suture well impressed; whorls 4, sides flat, the first large; aperture ovate, not fully developed; columellar margin vertical.

Size: maj. diam. 4·0; alt. axis 7·10 mm.

This shell, together with two specimens of *G. crassilabris*, was sent by me to Wm. Blanford many years ago, as recorded in his catalogue; its peculiar form was not noticed. I then put it on one side under the impression it was an accidental variety of some species. When going through the collection of *Glessulæ* collected by me in the Dafla Hills, Assam, I came on another specimen among some found on the Shengorh Peak, almost identical with the Khasi Hill shell. When one considers the enormous areas—in Assam, for instance—as yet unvisited by a conchologist, and compares them with the small scattered spots, miles apart, where often only a hurried search was possible, on one day in the year, there must be many a species yet to be discovered. More extensive diligent search in both the Khasi and Dafla Hills would lead, doubtless, to more specimens of this curious shell being found.

GLESSULA (JADUKAMIA) ABNORMIS, n. sp. (Plate CLX. fig. 23.)

Locality. Shengorh Peak, Dafla Hills. No. 3370 (*Godwin-Austen*).

Shell elongately ovate; sculpture fine, very regular raised ribbing; colour pale ochraceous; whorls 4, the first very ample; aperture ovate; columellar margin nearly vertical.

Size: maj. diam. 4·0; alt. axis 7·20 mm.

This *Glessula* is so distinct in shell character from all as yet known that I am induced to put it in a new subgenus, which I describe above.

6. *North Cachar, Naga Hills, and Manipur.*

Glessula burrailensis, G.-A.	Pl. CLX. figs. 1, 2.
burrailensis, var.	Pl. CLX. fig. 4.
burraliensis, var.	Pl. CLX. fig. 3.
burrailensis, var. *maxwelli*.	Pl. CLX. figs. 5, 6.
butleri, G.-A.	Pl. CLX. fig. 9.
illustris, G.-A.	Pl. CLX. fig. 12.
illustris, var. *tumida*, G.-A.	Pl. CLX. fig. 13.
stramencolor, n. sp.	Pl. CLIX. fig. 12.
manipurensis, n. sp.	{ Pl. CLIX. fig. 10. Pl. CLXIII. figs. 13, 13 a.
imphalensis, n. sp.	Pl. CLXII. fig. 24.
oglei, n. sp.	Pl. CLXII. fig. 10.
prowiensis, n. sp.	Pl. CLXII. fig. 13.
hebetata, n. sp.	Pl. CLXII. fig. 26.
barakensis, n. sp.	Pl. CLXII. figs. 12, 17.
lahupaensis, n. sp.	Pl. CLXI. fig. 23.
kohimaensis, n. sp.	Pl. CLXI. fig. 24.
shirohiensis, n. sp.	Pl. CLXI. fig. 21, 22.
lhotaensis, n. sp.	Pl. CLXI. fig. 25.
mastersi, n. sp. Type.	{ Pl. CLXII. fig. 1. Pl. CLXIII. figs. 20, 22.
mastersi, var.	Pl. CLXII. fig. 3.
macera, G.-A.	

GLESSULA (RISHETIA) BURRAILENSIS, G.-A. (Plate CLX. figs. 1, 2.) Type. No. 1722 B.M.

J. A. S. Bengal, xliv. 1875, p. 3, pl. i. fig. 6.

Locality. Khunho Peak, Naga Hills, Trigonometrical Station (*Godwin-Austen*).

Original Description :—" Shell turreted, elongate, solid, in fresh state brown and lustrous, finely longitudinally striated; whorls 10, rather flat, suture shallow, apex blunt; aperture subvertical, fusiform, angular above; peristome very thick, paler brown on margin; columella strong.

Alt. 1·37; major diam 0·4 in.

The finest specimens were collected under the Peak of Khunho, Eastern Burrail Range; they were also abundant under Japvo at about 7000 feet.

Size (Type, the largest): major diam. 9·5; length 33·8 mm· 100 : 41, spire to last whorl.

This beautiful species is found in the old damp and shady primaeval forest.

GLESSULA (RISHETIA) BURRAILENSIS, G.-A., var. (Plate CLX. fig. 4.) No. 1585 B.M.

Locality. Kopamedza Peak, 8375 ft., Naga Hills, Trigonometrical Station (*Godwin-Austen*).

Shell rather more tumid in form; colour ochraceous, with a strong green tint; whorls 8; columellar margin nearly straight, compared with type.

Size (specimen figured): major diam. 9·25; length 26·25 mm.

GLESSULA (RISHETIA) BURRAILENSIS, G.-A., var. (Plate CLX. fig. 3.) No. 1586 B.M.

Locality. Japvo Peak, Naga Hills, at 8–9000 feet (*Godwin-Austen*).

Shell much more slender in form; apex blunt, shining: sculpture well marked, regular striation, extending to the apex; colour strong ochraceous, with a greenish tint; spire elongate, sides flatly convex, suture impressed; whorls 9½; aperture ovate; peristome on outer margin slightly thickened; columellar margin slightly concave.

Size (specimen figured): major diam. 7·0: length 25·25 mm.

Plentiful in the forest, covering the Peak on all sides.

GLESSULA (RISHETIA) BUTLERI, G.-A. No. 1583 B.M. (Plate CLX. fig. 9.)

J. A. S. B. xliv. 1875, p. 4, pl. i. fig. 7.

Locality. Eastern Burrail Range (*Godwin-Austen*).

Original description :—" Shell elongately turreted, very thin and brittle, tumid, pale corneous, glassy, very minutely striated, apex very blunt; whorls 8, rather rounded, suture deep, body-whorl much swollen and capacious; aperture vertical, pear-shaped, lip rather thin.

" Alt. 1·13, major diam. 0·45 in.

" *Hab.* Eastern Burrail Range, at 6000 feet; not a common form.

" I name this shell after Captain J. Butler, Political Agent in the Naga Hills, with whom I had the fortune of being associated when mapping that very interesting and beautiful district."

Size : Largest specimen, major diam. 12·75; alt. axis 28·0 mm.
Specimen figured,   ,,   11·0;   ,,   26·25 ,,
Proportion of length to body-whorl, 100 : 54.

GLESSULA (RISHETIA) BURRAILENSIS, var. MAXWELLI. (Plate CLX. figs. 5, 6.) No. 1717 B.M.

Locality. Naga Hills, exact locality unknown, but East of Kohima (*Col. H. St. P. Maxwell*). Somra, Khulen Post, West of Kyendwin or Chindwin River, Upper Burma (*F. Ede*).

Shell elongately turreted; sculpture coarse, close, irregular ribbing (fig. 6); colour rich sienna-brown (fig. 6); spire long, sides nearly flat; 100 : 47·6; suture shallow: whorls 10, sides nearly flat; aperture narrowly oval, outer lip strong; columellar margin nearly straight, solid.

Size : Fig. 5. Type, major diam. 8·5 ; alt. axis 32·0 mm.
Largest bleached shell, ,, 9·2 ; ,, 35·0 ,,

This species was given to me by Colonel Maxwell ; obtained on one of his tours in the Naga Hills, East of the Anghami Naga tribe.

GLESSULA (RISHETIA) MASTERSI, n. sp. Type. (Plate CLXII. fig. 1.)

= *macera*, Nev. MS. from Assam.

Locality. Golaghat, Assam ; 3 specimens found. Blf. Coll. 843.06.1.1 B.M. (*Masters*). Same locality. 40.06.3. B.M., 2 examples ; 837.06.1.1 B.M., 5 examples.

Shell elongately turreted ; sculpture distant striation ; colour pale ochraceous ; spire long, sides flat ; apex is fine, increasing gradually (Pl. CLXIII. fig. 20 ; another specimen No. 837.06.1.1 B.M., Blf. Coll., from same locality, Pl. CLXIII. fig. 22), suture shallow ; whorls 9, very flatly convex : proportion of spire to last whorl 100 : 49, having a slight shoulder below the suture ; aperture rather narrow ; columellar margin nearly vertical.

Size : major diam. 6·5 ; length 17·5 mm. Largest specimen, apex broken, major diam. 7·0.

It is very close to *G. sarissa*, Bs., but side of spire differs.

This species was found in Dr. W. T. Blanford's collection and unnamed. It was sent to him with other shells found by Mr. Masters in 1860, on the low spurs near the hot spring at the Falls of the Namba River, the home of that fine species *Rhiostoma mastersi*, figured in the ' Conchologia Indica,' 1870, pl. v. fig. 1, without description, as *Pterocyclos (Spiraculum) mastersi*, Blanford MSS., afterwards described by Wm. Blanford in Journ. Asiat. Soc. Bengal, 1877, pt. 2, p. 313, as from hills south of the Assam Valley not far from Golaghat. Some years later I happened to encamp at the exact locality as given above. The shell is hairy in fresh specimens, as stated by Blanford.

Among the *Glessulæ* since recorded from the Indian Museum, under No. 80, Nevill, ' Hand-list,' p. 170, no. 3639, are some 12 examples of *mastersi* from Assam, labelled W. Blf. with the name " *macera* " in Nevill's handwriting. Writing to me in August 1880, Nevill gave this name to all the shells catalogued under No. 80. *G. macera* is a very distinct and attenuate species.

GLESSULA (RISHETIA) MASTERSI, n. sp., var. (Plate CLXII. fig. 3.) No. 3339 B.M.

Locality. Augaoluo Peak, 6777 ft., Naga Hills, 2 specimens (*M. Ogle*).

Sculpture : the embryonic whorls (Plate CLXII. fig. 21) are strongly costulate next the smooth apex, and regularly so to the last whorl ; colour dark umber-brown ; whorls 9.

Size : major diam. 7·0 ; alt. axis 20·0 mm.

Agrees with the Golaghat specimens.

5 other specimens were obtained in the Naga Hills ; precise locality not noted.

Glessula (Rishetia) macera, G.-A. W. Blf. MS. Type. No. 3673 B.M.

Locality. Assam, probably near Golaghat. *Ex* Coll. Indian Museum, No. 3634 (*W. T. Blanford*).

Shell elongately turreted, thin; sculpture regular, close subdued costulation; colour pale ochraceous; spire very long, sides flat; apex rather blunt; suture impressed; whorls 12, very gradually increasing, flatly convex, body-whorl short; aperture small; columellar margin flatly curved.

Size: major diam. 5·75; length 20·0 mm.

Under No. 68, ' Hand-list,' p. 169, Nevill records 10 specimens from Assam under *G. pertenuis*, presented by Stoliczka—a faulty determination; they are *G. macera,* and from the same source as No. 842.06.1.1 coll. Blf. B.M.

Glessula (Rishetia) stramencolor, n. sp. (Plate CLIX. fig. 12.)

Locality. Burrail Range. 6 specimens. Type. No. 1535 B.M. (*Godwin-Austen*).

Shell elongately turreted, thin, shiny; sculpture rather coarse, well-marked, regular transverse striation; colour very pale ochraceous, or straw-colour; spire long, side flat, apex very blunt; suture impressed; whorls 11, sides flat; aperture small, pear-shaped; peristome thin, outer lip vertical; columella curving downwards.

Size: major diam. 6·0; length 25·0 mm.

The general form and blunt apex of this species is more that of a *Bacillum* than of *Glessula.*

Glessula (Rishetia) imphalensis, n. sp. (Plate CLXII. fig. 24.)

Locality. Munipur. No. 3398 B.M. (*Godwin-Austen*).

Shell elongately turreted, with glassy surface; sculpture irregular striation; colour dull strong ochraceous; spire elongate, apex fine, sides very slightly convex; suture impressed; whorls 8, rather flattened; aperture narrowly oval; outer lip slightly thickened; columellar margin short, truncate, very slightly concave.

Size: Largest, major diam. 7·75; length 18·0 mm.
Ordinary, „ 7·50; „ 16–17 „

Glessula (Rishetia) munipurense, n. sp. (Plate CLIX. fig. 10.)

Locality. Munipur; over 20 specimens collected. Type. No. 1584 B.M. (*Godwin-Austen*).

Shell elongately turreted, thin, shiny; sculpture regular striation, showing strongly below the suture as a crenulate edge; colour pale umber-brown; spire long, sides with slight convexity; apex fine, blunt (Plate CLXIV. fig. 8, apex), as compared with *G. garoense* of Cachar (Plate CLXIV. fig. 7, No. 1657 B.M.); suture impressed; whorls 11, sides flatly convex; aperture small, subovate angular above and below ; peristome thin ; columella with rather a sharp turn, truncate below.

Size : major diam. 20·52 ; length 20·5 mm.

The sculpture distinguishes this species from *G. garoense*, small var., in being much coarser.

G. manipurense, n. sp., var. (3366 B.M.), Diyung Valley, Naga Hills, differs very slightly from the type.

GLESSULA SUBHASTULA, var.

Locality. Manipur. 3 specimens. No. 3572 B.M. (*Godwin-Austen*).

Shell elongately conoid ; sculpture well marked, some irregular striae : colour sienna-brown ; spire high, sides somewhat flat, apex rather blunt (Plate CLXIII. figs. 13, 13*a*) ; suture impressed ; whorls 8, sides flatly convex ; aperture narrow, almost straight on the outer margin : peristome a little thickened ; columellar margin slightly convex.

Size : major diam. 3·3 ; alt. axis 10·0 mm.

Differs slightly from the Khasi Hill form in being less attenuate, the sides of the spire being more convex above the larger body-whorl, more particularly in the sharper apex, which is very costulate throughout (Plate CLXIII. figs. 13, 13 *a*).

G. subhastula, n. sp. (No. 1591 B.M.), Lhota Naga Hills, four examples, similar to the type.

GLESSULA OGLEI, n. sp.   Type.   (Plate CLXII. fig. 10.)

Locality. Naga Hills. No. 820 B.M. (*M. T. Ogle*).

Shell elongate, oblong turreted ; sculpture regular striation ; colour bright ochraceous ; spire high, sides flatly convex ; suture well impressed ; whorls 7½, flatly convex ; aperture ovate ; peristome well thickened on outer margin ; columellar margin short and sharply concave.

Size : major diam. 5·5 ; length 14·0 mm.

Somewhat like *G. oakesi* of the Abor Hills, but more slender and attenuate, apex finer, and aperture more oval. More elongate than *G. crassilabris*, and the sculpture is not so incised as in that species and its varieties.

GLESSULA OGLEI, n. sp.   (Plate CLXII. fig. 11.)

Locality. Naga Hills. No. 3363 B.M. (*Godwin-Austen*).

Sculpture rather coarse striation, not incised ; whorls 7.

Size : major diam. 6·5 ; alt. axis 14·25 mm.

The figure of this species is somewhat more tumid than the type, but found with it are two quite similar ; they are not to be separated.

GLESSULA HEBETATA, n. sp.   (Plate CLXII. fig. 26.)

Locality. Munipur (*Godwin-Austen*).   No. 3396 B.M.

Shell oblong conoid ; sculpture irregular, rather close striation ; colour dull ochraceous brown ; spire elongately conic, sides flatly convex, apex blunt ; suture shallow ; whorls 6, rather flattened ; aperture narrowly oval ; peristome outer lip slightly thickened ; columellar margin short, slightly concave, terminating abruptly.

Size : maj. diam. 6·0 ; alt. axis 13 mm.

No. 1539 B.M. *hebetata*, n. sp., from the Burrail Range : larger than type, 16·5 × 7·5.

No. 3340 B.M. *hebetata*. n. sp., from the Augaoluo Peak, Naga Hills ; dark umber in colour.

GLESSULA BARAKENSIS, n. sp.   (Plate CLXII. fig. 12.)

Locality. Munipur, south of the Barak Valley (*Godwin-Austen*). Type. No. 3355 = 3349.

Shell elongately conoid, smooth to eye ; sculpture : fine, distant, regular, distinct striæ ; colour dull ochraceous : spire high, sides flattened ; suture moderately impressed ; whorls 7, sides very flatly convex, 100 : 58 ; aperture very narrowly ovate : peristome outer lip moderately thickened : columellar margin very slightly concave.

Size : maj. diam. 4·75 ; length 12·0 mm.

This is a common species in Munipur. I have it from Nongmaiching Peak (No. 3354 B.M. Coll.), from the Lahupa Naga Hills on the north-east (No. 821 B.M.), and from the Naga Hills, exact places unknown, but somewhere on the line of the Burrail Range. These last (No. 3364 B.M.), are rather shorter, more tumid, and of an umber-brown colour — 10 × 4·75 mm.

In the Beddome Collection (British Museum No. 753) were originally four specimens (now three) from the Naga Hills, no doubt received from Mr. Muspratt of the Assam Police—which Colonel Beddome had named *crassula*, Bs. : they agree with this species. *G. crassula*, Bs., does not extend to the Naga Hills—see what I say under that species.

GLESSULA BARAKENSIS, n. sp.   (Plate CLXII. fig. 17.)

Locality. Burrail Range, Naga Hills (*Godwin-Austen*).   No. 3349.

Shell ovately oblong. tumid ; sculpture regular, somewhat coarse striation, but not incised ; colour dull ochraceous : spire high, sides flatly convex, apex very blunt and rounded ; suture very well impressed ; whorls 6, decidedly convex ; aperture rather widely oval : peristome outer lip well thickened ; columellar margin convex just above the truncation.

Size : Type, maj. diam. 4·75 ; length 11·0 mm.

Rather smaller than the type.

There is one specimen from Tellizo Peak, Naga Hills (No. 3344 B.M.), near the watershed of the Burrail Range.

GLESSULA KOHIMAENSIS, n. sp.   (Plate CLXI. fig. 24.)

Locality. Kohima, Anghami Naga Hills, twelve examples (*Godwin-Austen*). Type. No. 3395 B.M.

Shell ovately oblong, slender, smooth, shiny ; sculpture : sparse, distant striæ ; colour dull ochraceous with green tinge ; spire high, curving on columellar side particularly ; suture impressed ; whorls 7, fairly convex ; aperture rather narrow, vertically oval ; peristome outer lip thickened ; columella gradually curving, truncate below.

Size : maj. diam. 3·75 ; alt. axis 9·75 mm.

GLESSULA PROWIENSIS, n. sp.   (Plate CLXII. fig. 13.)

Locality. Prowie. Lahupa, Naga Hills, N.E. Munipur, two specimens (*Godwin-Austen*). Type. No. 3565 B.M.

Shell elongately ovate, rather solid, glassy ; sculpture : very slight striation, distant ; colour pale greenish ; spire high, sides flatly convex, apex very blunt and rounded ; suture impressed ; whorls 6, sides slightly convex ; aperture narrowly ovate, vertical ; peristome outer lip thickened ; columellar margin short, straight, not truncate.

Size : maj. diam. 3·75 ; length 9·0 mm.

I have six other specimens from the Burrail Range (No. 1608 B.M.). From North Khasi Hills I collected two examples of a shell very like this (No. 3551), more ovate in form, with stronger truncate columella 8 mm. long, and with an ochraceous tint—this is *subhastula*.

It is very variab in size. Specimens from the Lahupa Naga Hills (No. 3378 B.M.) (Sikhami), six in number, are only 7 mm. in length ; of the same size are five from Tellizo Peak (No. 3345 B.M.). Was also found on Laisen Peak in Munipur.

No. 768 12.4.16 B.M. of the Beddome Collection is this species from the Naga Hills, five specimens no doubt collected by Mr. Muspratt. These were labelled by Colonel Beddome *G. orobia* ; placed in the box is a label in Mr. Gude's handwriting "1 *subjerdoni*," the four other specimens are *prowiensis*. See what I say under *G. orobia*.

No. 3356 B.M. *prowiensis* was collected south of the Barrail, Munipur.

No. 3362 B.M. *prowiensis* was collected on Khunho Peak, Naga Hills.

No. 3384 B.M. *prowiensis* was collected at Kezameh, Naga Hills.

GLESSULA SHIROBIENSIS, n. sp.   (Plate CLXI. fig. 22.)

Locality. Shiroifurar Trigonometrical Station, Lahupa Naga Hills (*Godwin-Austen*). Type. No. 3571 B.M.

Shell elongately conoid, rather solid ; sculpture regular, fairly strong striation ; colour ash-brown, paler on apex ; spire elongate, sides nearly flat, apex very blunt; suture impressed; whorls 6½, flatly convex; aperture narrowly oval, vertical, milky white inside; peristome thickened; columellar margin nearly vertical.

Size: Types............ maj. diam. 3·0; length 8·0 mm.
of larger bleached specimen, „ 3·25; „ 9·0 „

GLESSULA LHOTAENSE, n. sp. (Plate CLXI. fig. 25.)

Locality. Lhota Naga. Small, elongate (*Godwin-Austen*). No. 1590 B.M.

Shell elongately turreted; sculpture: distant irregular striation, with broad smooth intervals; colour pale ochraceous; spire high, apex blunt; suture well impressed; whorls 7½. sides flattened, proportion of length to body-whorl 100: 49; aperture narrowly elliptical; peristome thin; columellar margin perpendicular, nearly straight.

Size: maj. diam. 3·8; alt. axis 10·25 mm.

GLESSULA LAHUPAENSE, n. sp. (Plate CLXI. fig. 23.)

Locality. Phunggam, Lahupa Naga Hills (*Godwin-Austen*). Type. No. 3381 B.M.

Shell elongately turreted; sculpture regular, rather distant striæ; colour pale umber-brown; spire high, subulate, apex rounded, large, blunt; suture impressed; whorls 6, sides somewhat flattened, proportion 100 : 46; aperture oval, well rounded below, vertical; peristome outer lip thickened; columellar margin nearly perpendicular, with very slight curvature.

Size: maj. diam. 3·25; alt. axis 9·25 mm.

7. *Arakan and Chittagong.*

Glessula forum, n. sp.   Pl. CLXI. fig. 15.
rabani, n. sp.   Pl. CLX. fig. 21.

GLESSULA FORUM *, n. sp., is *naja*, G.-A., Blf. MS., not *naja* of Pilsbury from Assam, which is *subhebes*, G.-A. (Plate CLXI. fig. 15.)

Locality. Hathagori, north of Chittagong. *Ex* Hy. Blf. Coll., six specimens (*H. C. B. C. Rabau*). No. 14.9.3.15.

Shell elongate; sculpture: surface smooth, rather weak distant striation: colour ruddy ochraceous; spire long, sides slightly convex, tapering gradually to apex, then sharply at the 3 apical whorls; suture shallow: whorls 10, very slightly convex, proportion of spire to last whorl 56·2 : 100; aperture widely oval; columellar margin, with slight convexity.

Size: maj. diam. 7·5; length 22·25 mm.

* From the name of the place it came from, which means the "market village."

Approaches *G. tenuispira*, Bs., which has been recorded from Sylhet (probably the typical locality), from Pegu, Akouktoung, and farther south. This is a species which would have been likely by some of the early collectors to be considered *tenuispira*, but it does not agree either with Teria Ghat examples I have, nor with *Gless. mastersi* from Assam.

GLESSULA RABANI, n. sp. (Plate CLX. fig. 21.)

Locality. Chittagong. *Ex* Coll. Henry F. Blanford (*H. Raban*). No. 6.9.3.15.

Shell ovately conical, turreted ; sculpture : coarse distant striation partly incised ; colour rich sienna-brown; spire conic, sides slightly convex, apex blunt ; suture impressed ; whorls 7, sides flatly convex ; aperture narrowly oval ; peristome thickened on outer lip : columellar margin short, convex, thickened, truncate.

Size : maj. diam. 5·0 ; length 10·25 mm.

This is very close to *G. crassilabris*, but the spire is not so high, the aperture is narrower, and the coloration different from any specimens I have seen from the Khasi Hill Ranges. I name it after Mr. H. C. B. C. Raban, of the Indian Civil Service, who collected assiduously in the districts in which he served.

---

8. *Burmese.*

Glessula pertenuis, W. Blf.	Pl. CLXI. figs. 1, 2.
basseinensis, n. sp.	{ Pl. CLXI. fig. 3 { Pl. CLXIV. fig. 10.
nathiana, n. sp.	
akouktoungensis, n. sp.	
blanfordiana, Nevill.	Pl. CLXIV. fig. 21.
peguensis, W. Blf.	Pl. CLXII. figs. 20, 21.
ponsiensis, n. sp.	Pl. CLXIV. figs. 19, 20.

8 a. *Tenasserim.*

Glessula limborgi, n. sp.	Pl. CLXI. fig. 5.

GLESSULA PERTENUIS, W. Blf. (Plate CLXIV. fig. 11, apex; Plate CLXI. figs. 1, 2.)

Locality. Tongoop, Arakan ; and Henzada. No. 239.06.2.2. (*W. T. Blanford*).

Original description :—" *A. pertenuis*, n. sp. Shell very slender, turreted, thin, light horny, polished, closely, minutely, and rather irregularly striated. Spire subulate, somewhat acuminate towards the blunt apex; suture impressed, suberenulate. Whorls 11–12, convex, the last about 1/5 the length of the spire. Aperture oblique, ovately pyriform, peristome thin margins united by a thin callus, columella moderately curved, obliquely truncated.

	millim.	inch.
" Length	20	0·8.
Diameter	4½	0·18.
Length of aperture	4	0·16.

" *Habitat.* Tongoop, Arakan.

" Var. *major*, length 26½ mm.; diameter 6; length of aperture 6. Of another specimen; length 23 mm.; diameter 5⅔; length of aperture 5¼.

" *Habitat.* Pyema Khyoung, Bassein District, Pegu.

"A much more slender species than *A. tenuispira*, Bens. (a variety of which also abounds in parts of Pegu), though there are signs of a passage. The present appears to replace *A. tenuispira* in Arakan and Bassein. Mr. Benson, to whom I sent a specimen, observes that it is intermediate between *A. tenuispira* and *A. hastula*, Bens."

No. 239.06.2.2 of the Blanford collection is represented by seven examples of this species, with this pencil note by Blanford, "very like *tenuispira*," from two localities, Tongoop, in Arakan, and Henzada on the Irrawady, the respective locality was not indicated; but they are all alike, two are of the same length as given in the description—viz., 20 mm., white. The largest specimen now figured is 22·25 × 5 mm.

Fortunately I have from Henry Blanford's Collection (No. 20.9.3.15) two specimens from Henzada, one of which I figure; it is 22·0 mm. long × 5 in major diameter, which settles the matter of habitat. They no doubt were given him by his brother.

Under *G. pertenuis*, var. *major*, William Blanford gives the dimensions of a larger form from the Bassein District, which is farther to the south. Three examples from this locality are in the Henry Blanford collection; they do not agree with *pertenuis*, the general shape is different, the apex particularly being much blunter. It cannot be therefore considered a variety—I name and figure it as *G. basseinensis* (Plate CLXIV. fig. 10 for apex).

In Col. Beddome's Collection (No. 682) is a single large specimen, 26·75 in length × 7 mm., from Thyetmyo, named by him *G. baculina*; it agrees best with *G. nathiana*; it has much the general form of *pertenuis*, but is larger, is ash-coloured, with rough strong striation. A hasty examination recalls so-called *tenuispira* of Darjiling, but a closer shows quite a different increase of the whorls, and that they are by no means so flat. It is also milky white within the aperture, quite a distinguishing character, which I note is to be seen also in the typical specimen of *G. pertenuis* from Henzada. Nevill records *pertenuis* from Akouktoung and Thyetmyo. This large form must be the variety of *tenuispira* referred to by Wm. Blanford as abounding in parts of Pegu, and in his "Contributions to Indian Malacology," 1865, J. A. S. B. vol. xxxiv. p. 95, he says: " *Achatina tenuispira*, B., of small size, is common at Akouktoung and farther south."

On the same glass slip in the Blanford Collection (No. 238.06.2.2) were gummed five specimens, labelled *G. tenuispira*,

Pegu and Darjiling; four were certainly from the latter place, but one was quite a different species and smaller, and may have come from Pegu.

Nevill gives the Garo Hills on two specimens from my collection; this cannot be an accurate determination, as I have nothing like it. The ten specimens from Assam are something else.

Recently (July 1917) further material has come to hand: when going through Wm. Blanford's collection of duplicate shells, I came on four pill-boxes containing *Glessula* from Pegu, with true locality and named as follows:—

No. 1 contained *Achatina tenuispira* from Bassein District, 14 examples; No. 2 from Akouktoung, 18 examples; No. 3 *Achatina pertenuis* from Tongoop, which is on the Arakan Yoma, 3 examples; No. 4 " intermediate between *tenuispira* and *pertenuis* " from Pyema Khyoung, Bassein District, 20 examples. These clear up doubts on distribution and show so well what Blanford's views were at the time he was describing Pegu Glessulas. No. 4 is *G. basseinensis*, described further on. No. 2 differs from this in many respects, due, no doubt, to its habitat on the Limestone rocks, which the name implies, " Akonk " being lime and " toung " a hill in Burmese; I remember the place well. I adopt it as the specific name. No 1 is a well-defined species differing from the preceding, which I name *G. nathiana*, from the Burmese name " nath " for spirits or fairies of woods and hills.

GLESSULA BASSEINENSIS, n. sp.   (Plate CLXIV. fig. 12. apex; Plate CLXI. fig. 3.)

Locality. Bassein. Pegu, three specimens. Pyema Khyoung, Bassein, six specimens (*W. T. Blanford*). Type. No. 19.9.3.15 B.M.

Shell elongately turreted; sculpture close, fine, regular, rather coarse; colour ochraceous; spire elongate, sides nearly straight, very slightly acuminate near the blunt apex, 100 : 33·7; suture moderately impressed; whorls 11, sides very flatly convex; aperture narrowly ovate; columellar margin curved slightly.

Size: major diam. 6·25; alt. axis 25·0 mm.

This is the var. *major* of *pertenuis* Blanford alluded to above; it is not so attenuate in general form, the apex is much stronger and blunter, fewer whorls, white, longer, and the sculpture coarser; a comparison of figure (No. 3) with those of true *tenuispira* from Teria Ghat and *hastula* shows, better than any description, how much it differs.

GLESSULA (RISHETTIA) NATHIANA, n. sp.

Locality. Bassein District (*W. T. Blanford*). Type. No. 2206 06.1.1 B.M.

Shell elongately turreted; sculpture regular, fine, raised, close striæ throughout; colour strong, ochraceous; spire elongate, sides nearly flat, apex very blunt ; suture well impressed ; whorls 11, sides flatly convex ; aperture broadly ovate ; columellar margin very convex.

Size : maj. diam. 7·0 ; length 22·75 mm.

This species was found among Blanford's duplicate shells, the box marked with above locality and with the note "intermediate between *tenuispira* and *pertenuis*"; it differs quite sufficiently from both and from *basseinensis* to be distinguished. From the last, it is far longer at the body-whorl, which is very swollen, its sides more convex, and the apex is much larger.

GLESSULA AKOUKTOUNGENSIS, n. sp.

Locality. Akouktoung on Irawady, Pegu (*W. T. Blanford*). Type. No. 2207.06.1.1 B.M.

Shell elongately turreted ; sculpture scarcely any, just a trace near apex below the suture; colour umber-brown; spire long, sides flat, apex blunt; suture impressed ; whorls 10, sides flatly convex ; aperture ovate.

Size : maj. diam. 5·75 ; length 20·5 mm.

This species occurred among the duplicates in the Blanford Collection. Compared with *G. basseinensis*, it differs in sculpture, in colour, and the last whorl is more tumid in proportion to the length.

GLESSULA PEGUENSIS, W. Blf.   (Plate CLXII. figs. 20, 21.)

Locality. Pegu.   No. 8.9.3.15 (*Hy. Blanford*).

Original description :—" *A. peguensis*, n. sp. Shell oblong ovate, rather solid, dark reddish brown, horny, marked with distinct and regular impressed lines. Spire convexly conical : apex obtuse ; suture impressed, suberenulate. Whorls 6½, slightly convex : the last ascending a little towards the mouth, and exceeding ⅓ of the shell in length : aperture vertical, truncately semicircular ; peristome obtuse, slightly thickened : margins joined by a callus ; columella very much curved, projecting forwards at the base, sub-vertically truncated within the peristome.

	millim.	inch.
" Length	7	0·28.
Diameter	3½	0·14.
Length of aperture	2¾	0·11.

" *Habitat.* Irawady Valley, Pegu: common.

" A pretty little species, darker in colour than any of its allies, except perhaps *A. gemma*, Bens., and easily distinguished from all, by the columella being more arcuate, also by its more acuminate spire and blunter apex, and its much stronger sculpture."

I give two figures of this shell, from authentic specimens in Hy. Blanford's Collection, as there is some variation in form.

In the Blanford Collection (No. 262.06.2.2) are three specimens from Arakan, near Tongoop, much larger than the type described, being 10 × 4·8 mm., but they do not differ in any other respect, and may be considered a large variety.

GLESSULA PONSIENSIS, n. sp.   (Plate CLXIV. fig. 19, apex.)

Locality. Ponsee, Yunnan.   Coll. Indian Museum (*Dr. John Anderson*).

Shell oblong turreted, solid, smooth to eye; apex very rounded with flattened sides; sculpture: none discernible on the two apical whorls, slight striæ on 3rd regularly, distantly, and finely costulate on the 4th; colour pale ochraceous; spire tapering, apex blunt, sides very slightly convex; suture shallow: whorls 9, sides flatly convex; aperture ovate, vertical; peristome somewhat thickened; columellar margin strong, concave.

Size: maj. diam. 7·75; alt. axis 20·0 mm.

This is *Stenogyra (Glessula) pyramis*, Bs., var. *major*, of Nevill, 'Hand-list,' i. p. 169, referred to under *G. pyramis* by me. I am fortunate in getting the type-shells for examination. I always doubted the extension of *G. pyramis* so far to the eastward, when it had never occurred in the Naga Hills or Munipur, or even Eastern Assam.

Glessula blanfordiana, Nevill: Ponsee (*Dr. J. Anderson*). I am able to state that this is No. 85 of Nevill's 'Hand-list,' p. 171, as entered in Geoffrey Nevill's amended copy in his own handwriting: that he did not at that time consider it had any close relationship to *G. peguensis*, is shown by the two lines crossed out, and " 6, Loc ? coll. W. Theobald." Bhamao. is entered as the habitat.

The type from Ponsee, Yunnan (Plate CLXIV. fig. 20, apex), has been sent me from Calcutta by the Director of the Zoological Survey of India, Dr. N. Annandale, with one other example. This type is, I should say, abnormally thickened, particularly on the columella and tip of the peristome. Nevill's description is excellent.

I closely compared these with the specimens also collected by Dr. John Anderson at Bhamao (Plate CLXIV. fig. 21, apex), six in number, and made drawings of their respective species, which show considerable variation not amounting to specific difference.

The sculpture of the Ponsee shell is distinctly costulate, while it is very finely so in those from Bhamao (Plate CLXIV. fig. 21. apex), and this extends to the whole apex, as in the type (fig. 20).

As *Glessula peguensis* has been referred to as an allied species, I compared and figured the apex, which is of very different form and sculpture (Plate CLXIV. fig. 22, apex)—the specimen selected being one in the Wm. Blanford Collection from Tongoop, Arakan.

GLESSULA LIMBORGI, n. sp.   (Plate CLXI. fig. 5.)

Locality. Tenasserim (*Ossian Limborg*).

Shell elongately turreted, with shining surface; sculpture: very regular striation, less apparent on the last whorl; colour rich umber with a green tinge; spire elongate, sides nearly flat; apex somewhat attenuated, blunt; suture shallow; whorls 11, increasing very gradually in size, sides flattened, the last with a sign of a keel above the aperture; aperture rather narrow, ovate, straight on inner margin; outer lip flatly convex; columellar margin sharply convex, then straight not solid, feeble truncation.

Size: maj. diam. 6·5; alt. axis 26 mm.

This single specimen was among the shells collected by Mr. O. Limborg in 1877, and I name it after him; it has remained undescribed ever since. The species is of delicate form, and quite distinct from any *Glessula* I have from Pegu.

Mr. Ossian Limborg was a particularly fine strong young man, son of a Swedish minister, and a keen naturalist. He arrived in Calcutta in the winter of 1876, and called on me one morning at the Museum anxious to collect and explore anywhere. I took him up, and together with Lord Tweeddale, Dr. John Anderson, Superintendent of the Indian Museum, and Mr. Wood Mason, we fitted him out with all that was necessary and sent him to Moulmein to collect in Tenasserim, from whence he returned in May 1877, with an interesting lot of Birds, Mollusca, and Insects, which he was instructed to pay particular attention to. Very much material was obtained on the Peak of Mooleyit and its vicinity; of the mollusca he brought back were some very interesting and valuable species preserved in spirits. I am sorry to say he suffered much from malarial fever and had to return to Europe, otherwise he was to have been employed in some other parts of Burma.

7 a. *Shan States and Siam Frontier.*

Glessula kentungensis, n. sp.	
woodthorpi, n. sp.	Pl. CLXII. fig. 19.
yuenagensis, n. sp.	Pl. CLXII. fig. 18.
feddeni, n. sp.	Pl. CLXI., fig. 15.
feddeni, var.	Pl. CLXII. fig. 14.
ineditus, n. sp.	
perlevis, n. sp.	

GLESSULA KENTUNGENSIS, n. sp.

Locality. Mong Sing, Siam Boundary (*Lt.-Col. R. Woodthorpe, R.E.*). Type. No. 3650 B.M.

Shell elongately turreted; sculpture: smooth, with irregular subdued ribbing, showing stronger and curvilinear below the suture, apex quite smooth, faint sculpture on 2nd and 3rd whorls; colour dull ochraceous; spire elongate, flat-sided, apex very blunt, large ; suture well impressed ; whorls 9, sides nearly flat ; aperture small, ovate ; columellar margin very convex.

Size : maj. diam. 8·0 ; length 30·25 mm.

This species was also found on the Mekong River, paler in colour, with an ashy tint.   No. 3748 B.M.

GLESSULA WOODTHORPEI, n. sp.   (Plate CLXII. fig. 19.)

Locality. Shan States. Nine specimens (*Lt.-Col. R. Woodthorpe*). Type. No. 1628 B.M.

Shell oblong conoid, shiny, very smooth ; sculpture : distant, rather coarse indistinct irregular striæ ; colour olivaceous ; spire elongately conic, apex blunt ; suture well impressed ; whorls 7, gradually increasing, body-whorl to length 100 : 55·6 ; aperture ovate, vertical ; peristome outer tip thickened ; columellar margin slightly concave, short, strong, truncate.

Size : maj. diam. 5·75 ; length 13·5 mm.

This shell has a likeness to *G. crassilabris*, but the aperture is smaller in proportion to the length ; it is not so pointed in the spire, and the sculpture is different.

A specimen (bleached) No. 3655, is from the Siam N.W. boundary.

GLESSULA FEDDENI, n. sp.   (Plate CLXII. fig. 15.)

Locality. Shan Hills (*Wm. Blanford coll.*). Type. No. 261.06.2.2.

Shell elongately conoid, tumid, very glassy ; sculpture : rather distant striation, closer and stronger on the apical whorls ; colour rich ochre ; spire conic, flatly convex, apex blunt ; suture impressed ; whorls 7, sides convex, the last very ample ; aperture oval ; peristome outer lip thickened ; columellar margin short, with considerable convexity.

Size : maj. diam. 6·75 ; alt. axis 13·2 mm.
          „   „   6·0 ; „   „ 14·75 mm.

This is the shell Blanford refers to as perhaps distinct from *crassilabris*, Bens., J. A. S. B. 1865, p. 95 ; it much resembles that species, but placed side by side the points of variation are readily seen.   Another single specimen (No. 41.06.33.) occurs in the Blanford collection, much more slender in form, but with similar sculpture, which I consider a variety (Plate CLXIII. fig. 14).

GLASSULA INEDITUS, n. sp.

Locality. Shan Hills. Three specimens not named (*W. T. Blanford collection*). Type. No. 88.06.5.5.

Shell oblong turreted ; sculpture : transverse close regular raised striation, embryonic whorls smooth ; colour : the type and best preserved rich ochraceous on last whorl ; spire elongate, sides flat ; suture impressed ; whorls 7, regularly increasing, slightly convex ; aperture ovate, small ; peristome outer margin thickened ; columellar margin short, terminating abruptly.

Size : maj. diam. 4·5 ; alt. axis 9·5 mm.

This species was found quite recently (July 1919) in a pill-box labelled "Shan Hills," together with another very distinct species and a *Bithynia*, July 1919. It thus remained unsorted and unnoticed for so many years, until my attention was called to the Mollusca of the Salween Valley.

GLESSULA PERLEVIS, n. sp.

Locality. Shan Hills, five specimens (2 mature) (*W. T. Blanford collection*). Type. No. 89.06.5.6.

Shell ovately oblong: sculpture: smooth on last whorl, only a trace of transverse striation on other whorls, and distant, high-power, close, spiral striation ; colour dull umber-brown ; spire short, sides flatly convex, apex rounded, very blunt ; suture impressed : whorls 6, flatly convex, last the largest ; aperture ovate or semicircular, outer margin evenly convex, vertical : peristome outer lip thickened ; columellar margin short, strong, concave.

Size : maj. diam. 4·75 ; alt. axis 9·5 mm.

This species recalls *G. pequensis* in its shape and blunt apex, but its colour and great smoothness distinguishes it at once. It probably comes from the Shan States near Mandalay and was collected by Fedden.

GLESSULA YUANGENSIS, n. sp.   (Plate CLXII. fig. 18.)

Locality. Yuang Ha, Siam boundary, only one specimen (*Lt.-Col. R. Woodthorpe*).

Shell oblong turreted or conoid ; sculpture : strong regular distant striæ, approaching costulation ; colour ochraceous ; spire elongately conic, apex very blunt and rounded ; suture impressed ; whorls 7, sides flatly convex, 100 : 47 ; aperture narrowly ovate ; peristome outer lip thickened ; columellar margin very slightly convex, strongly truncate.

Size : maj. diam. 6 ; alt. axis 12·8 mm.

I was at first inclined to consider this a variety of *woodthorpei*, but it differs in many respects, in the proportion of the body-whorl to the height, the strong sculpture as compared with the smoothness and the difference in the aperture. A single bleached shell from the Kentung State (No. 1156 B.M.) is near this.

GLESSULA LATESTRIATA, Möllendorff.

Locality. Shan States.

This I have never seen.

GLESSULA (RISHETIA) SUNDERI, n. sp.

Locality. Amin Gaon, Gowhathi, Assam. Only one example (*Sunder Lall Hora*). Type in Indian Museum, Calcutta.

Shell very elongately turreted; sculpture: smooth to eye, rather distant striation in low relief, the first two embryonic whorls smooth; colour pale umber-brown; spire long, very regularly tapering, apex fine; suture well impressed; whorls 14, sides flatly convex, proportion of last whorl to length, 100 : 32·5; aperture narrowly ovate; peristome simple, thin; columellar margin concave, sharply truncate.

Size: maj. diam. 9·5; alt. axis 41·5 mm.

This is a beautiful and new species, the single specimen is in most perfect state. Its nearest ally is *G. baculina*, Hy. Blandford, of Darjiling, compared with which it differs in its greater length and number of whorls, 14 to 13, and general tumidity, more convex whorls, with suture more impressed, sculpture not so full, side of spire not so straight and flat, last whorl larger and more swollen.

Compared with *G. subaculina*, G.-A., of the Khasi Hills and South Jaintia, another near ally, it differs considerably as follows: It is much longer, 14 whorls to 12, length 41 to 34·75 mm.; more alternate with finer apex; tapering very regularly, side of spire quite straight; sculpture far less pronounced; columellar margin shorter and with more convexity. Considerable interest is attached to the finding of this *Glessula* at Amin Gaon, 400 yards from the Railway Station, where Sunder Lall of the Indian Museum, returning from Munipur, was detained for six hours; he made the best of the opportunity, obtaining at the same time six specimens of another *Glessula*, a variety of *sarissa*.

Regarding the range of *G. baculina*, it is of interest; 400 miles east of Darjiling, at the base of the Dafla Hills, 450 feet, I found that *G. haemultiensis* took its place; the apex is more obtuse and the sculpture is very different from that of Hy. Blandford's species. It comes from a low elevation compared with Darjiling; Harmutti is some 150 miles east from Gowhathi; 50 miles north of that place, near Dewangiri, at the base of the Bhutan Hills, the Dafla species, or one very close to it, in all probability is to be found, indicative of the area and side from which *G. sunderi* was derived. The intrusive granite at Gowhathi extends thence for some distance north, exposed and rising at intervals above the deep alluvial of the Bramaputra, which evidently covers much more, pointing to a once close connection of low hilly country, by which land-mollusca could travel far out into the plain of Assam. Such former connection with the Assam Range or the Khasi and Garo Hills is more pronounced between Gowhathi and Dubri, trending towards the great mass of granite of Gipmochi Peak into the Western Bhutan Hills (see also page 11).

I have not hitherto seen any elongate *Glessula* (*Rishetia*) of the *baculina* type from so low an elevation as Gowhathi (only about 300 feet) and so far from the base of the eastern Himalaya, all have come from quite high habitats of 3-5000 feet. This is not surprising when we consider that from Gowhathi westward up to the Garo Hills, an area of 135 miles by 32, or over 4100 sq miles, no land-mollusca have been collected, until the high ground in the Khasi Hills is reached, where *G. subbaculina* is abundant. Eastward it is the same up to the Mikir Hills, a tract mostly of hill-country, 64 miles long by 32 broad or some 2000 sq. miles. North of the Brahmaputra, for the distance of 190 miles, another 6000 sq. miles, no collecting has been made. I trust Sunder Lall will before long be given the opportunity of collecting all along the line of the Assam railway and visit places contiguous to it, particularly the isolated low granite hills north of the Brahmaputra River.

GLESSULA BURRAILENSIS, G.-A., var. MAXWELLI, G.-A.

Locality. Somra Tracts, Somra Khulen Post, Upper Burma, S.E.19. About L. 25° 20' N., L. 90° 45' E. No. 3742 B.M.

Shell elongate cylindro-conoid, turreted, solid, rather shining; sculpture : on the protoconch ribbing, approaching fine costulation, merges into finer, more irregular, and curvilinear on the succeeding whorls ; just below the suture this sculpture is stronger, giving the appearance of crenulation ; colour a rich ochre, some are chestnut ; spire long, gradually increasing, sides with slight convexity, apex blunt ; suture moderately impressed ; whorls 10½, flatly convex, the last the largest ; aperture oval, rather narrow for size, milky white within ; peristome outer margin well thickened, white ; columella strong, concave, truncate.

Size :   maj. diam. 10·0 ; alt. axis 32·75 mm.

The longest and }   „   „   9·25 ;   „   „   33·5 mm.
most attenuate }

This very interesting shell was collected by Captain L. R. Mawson, 1st Lushai Hills Battalion, Assam Rifles, and is a more attenuate form of *G. burrailensis* from the Naga Hills, this easterly locality extending the range to the hill-slopes of the Kyengdwen Valley.

62

LAND AND FRESHWATER

EXPLANATION OF PLATE CLIX.

Fig. 1. *Glessula (Rishetia) longispira,* n. sp.   Rishettehu, Sikhim,   × 1·25.
2. — (—) · —, n. sp.   Rushehu, Sikhim.   × 1·50.
3. — (——) *tenuispira,* Bs.   Teria Ghat, Khasi.   × „
4. — (——) *subaculina,* n. sp.   Khasi Hills.   × „
5. — (——) *harmuttiensis,* n. sp.   Dafla Hills.   × „
6. — — (——) *rissomensis,* n. sp.   Damsang, Sikhim.   × ··
7. —— (——) *baculina,* H. Blf. (Type).   Darjiling.   × 1·5.
8. —— (——) *canaraense,* n. sp.?   N. Canara.   × 1·25.
9. —— (——) *subaculina,* n. sp.   North Khasi.   × 1·50.
10. —— (——) *manipurense,* n. sp.   Manipur.   × „
11. —— (——) *garoense,* n. sp., small var.   Naraindhur, Cachar.   × „
12. —— (——) *stramencolor,* n. sp.   Naga Hills.   × „
13. —— (——) *baculina,* H. Blf., var., *exilis.*   Damsang, Sikhim.   × „
14. —— (——) ——, „ „. (Type).   Rissom Peak, Sikhim.   × „
15. —— (——) *garoense,* n. sp. (Type).   Garo Hills.   × „

EXPLANATION OF PLATE CLX.

Fig. 1. *Glessula (Rishetia) burrailensis,* G.-A.
     (Type). KhunhoPk.,Naga Hills. × 1·25.
2. — (——) ——.   „ „   × „
3. — (——) ——.   Japvo Pk., „   × „
4. — (——) ——.   Kopamedza Pk., „   × „
5. — (——) *maxwelli,* n. sp. (1st Type).   Naga Hills.   × „
6. — (——) ——. (2nd Type).   „   × „
7. — (——) *dikrangense,* n. sp.   Dafla Hills.   × 1·50.
7 a. — (——) ——.   „   × „
8. — *ochracea,* n. sp.   Sikhim.   × „
9. — *butleri,* G.-A.   Naga Hills.   × „
10. — *moiumensis,* n. sp. (Type).   Patkai Range.   × „
11. — ——, n. sp. (Type).   Singpho Hills.   × „
12. — *illustris,* G.-A. (Type).   Hengdan Peak, Naga.   × „
13. — ——, var. *tumida,* G.-A.   Jaintia.   × „
14. — *crassilabris,* Bs.   N. Khasi.   × 2.
15. — *oakesi,* n. sp.   Abor Hills.   × 1·50.
16. — ——.   Bramakund, E. Assam.   × „
17. — *crassilabris,* Bs. (Typical).   Teria Ghat, Khasi.   × 2.
18. — ——.   Jaintia Hills.   × „
19. — ——.   Shengork Peak,   × „
       Dafla Hills.
20. — ——.   Garo Hills.   × „
21. — *rubani,* n. sp.   Chittagong.   × „
22. — (*Jadukamia*) *abnormis,* n. sp.   Khasi Hills.   × 3.
23. — (——) ——.   Dafla Hills.   × „
24. — *pyramis,* Bs.   Teria Ghat, Khasi.   × 1·50.

EXPLANATION OF PLATE CLXI.

Fig. 1. *Glessula (Rishetia) pertenuis,* W. Blf.   Pegu.   × 1·5.
2. — (——) ——.   Henzada, Pegu.   × „
3. — (——) *basseinensis,* n. sp.   Bassein, „   × „
4. — (——) *pertenuis,* W. Blf., large var.   Thyetmyo.   × „
5. — (——) *limborgi,* n. sp.   Tenasserim.   × ··
6. — (——) *sublebes,* n. sp. (Type).   Dafla Hills.   × 2.
7. — (——) ——.   Naga.   × 1·5.
8. — (——) ——.   Assam.   × „
9. — (——) ——.   Kohliagur,   × „
       near Tezpur, Assam.

Fig. 10. *Glessula (Rishetia) sarissa*, Bs.   Lower Bengal.   × 2.
   11. —— (——) *nevilliana*, n. sp.   Dafla Hills.   × „
   12. —— (——) ——.   „   „   × „
   13. —— (——) ——.   „   „   × 2·5.
   14. —— (——) *mastersi*, n. sp.   „   „   × 2.
   15. —— (——) *forum*, n. sp.   Chittagong.   × 1·5.
   16. —— (——) *hastula*, Bs.   Darjiling.   × 2.
   17. —— (——) —— (Typical).   „   × „
   18. —— (——) *subhastula*, n. sp. (Type).   North Khasi.   × „
   19. —— (——) ——, var. (Type).   „   × „
   20. —— (——) ——, „   „   Munipur.   × „
   21. —— (——) *shiroiensis*, n. sp.   „   × „
   22. —— (——), n. sp.   „   × „
   23. —— (——) *lahupaensis*, n. sp.   „   × „
   24. —— (——) *kohimaensis*, n. sp.   Naga Hills.   × „
   25. —— (——) *lhotaensis*, n. sp.   Lhota, Naga Hills.   × „
   26. ——   ⎧ *gemma*, Bo.   Khoostia, Bengal.   × „
   27. —— (sub-genus?) ⎨   „   Bengal (authentic).   × „
   28. ——   ⎪   „   Chandanagur.   × „
   29. ——   ⎩   „   var.   Chittagong.   × „

EXPLANATION OF PLATE CLXII.

Fig. 1. *Glessula (Rishetia) mastersi*, n. sp. (Type). Assam.   × 1·50.
   2. —— (——) *subhebes*, G.-A. (var. *tumida*). Golaghat, Naga.   × „
   3. —— (——) ——,   „   Naga.   × „
   4. —— (——) *aborensis*, G.-A.   Abor Hills.   × „
   5. —— *orobia*, Bs.   Darjiling.   × 2.
   6. —— —— (Type).   „   × „
   7. —— —— (var. *major*).   Richila Pk., Sikhim.   × 1·5.
   8. —— *solida*, n. sp.   North Khasi.   × 2.
   9. —— *crassula*, Bs., var.   Sikhim.   × „
   10. —— *oglei*, n. sp.   Naga Hills.   × 1·50.
   11. ——.   „   × „
   12. —— *barakensis*, n. sp.   Munipur (Type).   × „
   13. —— *prowiensis*, n. sp.   „   „   × 1·50.
   14. —— *feddeni*, n. sp., var.   Shan States.   × 1·50
   15. —— ——, „   „   „   × „
   16. —— *hanleyi*, n. sp.   North Khasi.   × 2.
   17. —— *barakensis*, n. sp.   Naga.   × „
   18. —— *yuangensis*, n. sp.   Shan States.   × 1·5.
   19. —— *woodthorpei*, n. sp.   „   „   × „
   20. —— *peguensis*, W. Blf.   Thyetmyo, Pegu.   × 2.
   21. ——.   „   „   × „
   22. —— *crassilabris*, Bs. (var. *nana*).   North Khasi.   × 2.
   23. —— *rarhiensis*, n. sp.   Sikhim.   × 1·5.
   24. —— *imphalensis*, n. sp.   Munipur.   × „
   25. —— *crassula*, Rve. (Type).   Darjiling.   × 2.
   26. —— *hebitata*, n. sp.   Munipur.   × 1·5.

EXPLANATION OF PLATE CLXIII.

(Enlargements of original Drawings.)

Fig. 1. *Glessula botellus*, Bs.   Nilghiris.   × 12·5.
   2. —— *oakesi*, G.-A. (Type).   Abor Hills.   × „
   3. —— *botellus*, Bs., of Preston.   „   × „
   4. —— *prowiensis*, n. sp. (*orobia*, Beddome). Naga Hills.   × „
   5. —— *subjerdoni* Bedd. (var. *minor*, *sub-*   Jeypur.   × „
         jerdoni of Nevill).
   6. —— ——.   Tinnevelly Hills.   × „
   7. —— ——.   Golconda.   × „

Fig. 8.	*Glessula orobia*, Bs.	Darjiling.	× 12·5.
9.	—— (*Rishetia*) *hastula*, Bs.	„	× „
9 a.	—— (——) —— (apex more enlarged).	„	× 24.
10.	—— (——) *roberti*, n. sp.	Richila, Sikhim.	× „
11.	—— (——) *subhastula*, n. sp.	North Khasi.	× 12·5.
12.	—— (——) —— (var.).	North Cachar.	× „
12 a.	—— (——) ——.	„	× 24.
13.	—— (——) *subhastula*, var.	Munipur.	× 12·5.
13 a.	—— (——) ——.	„	× 24.
14.	—— *subhastula*, n. sp.	Cherra Poonjee, Khasi.	× „
15.	—— —— (Type).	North Khasi.	× 24.
16.	—— (*Rishetia*) *sarissa*, Bs. (var.).	Burroi Gorge, Dafla.	× 12·5.
17.	—— (——) —— (var.).	Gowhathi.	× „
18.	—— (——) —— (Typical).	Jessore.	× „
19.	—— (——) —— (var.).	Koliaghur, Tezpur, Assam.	× „
20.	—— (——) *mastersi*, n. sp. (Type).	Golaghat, Assam.	× „
21.	—— (——) —— (var.).	Angaolno Pk., Naga.	× „
22.	—— (——) ——.	Golaghat, Assam.	× „

EXPLANATION OF PLATE CLXIV.

(Original drawings all × 12·5 and reduced ¼.)

Fig. 1.	*Glessula subhebes* (Type).	Dafla Hills.
2.	—— ——.	Abor Hills.
3.	—— *austeniana*, Nevill (Type).	Dafla.
4.	—— (*Rishetia*) *dihingensis*, n. sp.	Sonari Tea Garden, Assam.
5.	—— (——) *garoense*, n. sp. (Type).	Garo Hills.
6.	—— (——) —— (small var.).	Cachar.
7.	—— (——) *macera*, W. Blf. MS. (Type).	Assam.
8.	—— —— *munipurensis* (Type).	Munipur.
9.	—— *prowiensis*.	Naga Hills.
10.	—— (*Rishetia*) *pertenuis* (large var.).	Thyetmyo, Pegu.
11.	—— (——) ——.	Pegu.
12.	—— (——) *basseinensis*, n. sp.	Bassein, Pegu.
13.	—— *crassula* (large var.).	Darjiling.
14.	—— —— (Typical).	„
15.	—— —— (var. with incised lines).	Rarhichu, Sikhim.
16.	—— *crassilabris*, Bs.	Teria Ghat, Khasi.
17.	—— ——.	Dafla Hills.
18.	—— —— (small var.).	Naga Hills.
19.	—— *ponsiensis*, n. sp. *pyramis* (var. major). Nevill.	Ponsee, Yunnan.
20.	—— *blanfordiana* (Type), × 12.	„
21.	—— ——, × 12.	Bamao, Burma.
22.	—— *peguensis*, W. Blf.	Arakan.
23.	—— *pyramis*, Bs.	Teria Ghat.

EXPLANATION OF PLATE CLXV.

Glessula (*Rishetia*) *longispira*, n. sp.   Risetchu, Sikhim.

Fig. 1.   Aperture, with foot protruding, × 8.

        [*rdl–ldl*, right and left dorsal lobes. *cp*, fleshy columellar pillar upon and around which the columellar margin is built. *s*, peristome.]

1 a.   Generative organs, × 4·5.

1 b.   Penis of 2nd specimen examined.

1 c.   The visceral sac, showing coils, back and front views.

Glessula ochracea, G.-A.   Sikhim.

2 A. Aperture with foot protruding, showing sole of foot, × 4.
2 B. Buccal mass, with intestine and salivary glands, × 8.
2 C. Genitalia nearly complete, × 4·5.

Glessula oakesi, G.-A.   Abor Hills.

3 A. Side of foot, × 6.
3 B. Albumen gland, hermaphrodite duct, and oviduct to vas deferens,×6.
3 C. Vas deferens to penis, × 6.
3 D.   ,,   ,,   another view, × 6.

Glessula orobia, Bs.

4.   Generative organs, × 8.
4 a. Penis, with flagellum, × 12.
4 b.   ,,   another view, × 8.

Glessula inornata, Pfr.

5.   Part of genitalia, × 4·5.
5 a.   ,,   ,,   another view, × 4·5.
5 b. Penis, coiled view of, × 4·5.
5 c. Jaw, × 24.

Glessula garoense, n. sp.   Silchar, Cachar.

6.   Penis, with simple flagellum, × 12.
6 a. Spermatheca, × 12.

Glessula species ?   Buddula, Ceylon.

7.   Penis, to show flagellum, × 8.
7 a.   ,,   view of other side, × 8.
7 b. Follicles of the prostate, × 24.

www.ingramcontent.com/pod-product-compliance
Lightning Source LLC
Chambersburg PA
CBHW022021080426
42733CB00007B/669